Cinderellas
&
Packhorses

Cinderellas & Packhorses
A History of the Shropshire Magistracy

edited by

David J. Cox and Barry S. Godfrey

Logaston Press

LOGASTON PRESS
Little Logaston Woonton Almeley
Herefordshire HR3 6QH
logastonpress.co.uk

First published by Logaston Press 2005
Copyright © the authors 2005

ISBN 1 904396 45 3

Set in Times New Roman by Logaston Press
and printed in Great Britain by
Cromwell Press, Trowbridge

*Front cover illustration: Bridgnorth Town Hall
(which contains the town's courthouse)*

Contents

Contributors

Professor Roger Swift is Head of Department at the Centre for Victorian Studies, University College, Chester

Dr. David C. Cox is a Fellow of Keele University and a leading contributor to the *Victoria County History of Shropshire.*

Mr. David J. Cox MA is a Research Assistant in the School of Criminology, Education, Sociology & Social Work, Keele University

Dr. Helen Johnston is a Lecturer in Criminology, Department of Social Policy and Criminology, University of Hull

Dr. Barry Godfrey is a Senior Lecturer in the School of Criminology, Education, Sociology & Social Work, Keele University

Editors

Dr. Godfrey is a leading academic in Criminology as well as a serving Justice of the Peace, and has had numerous articles published in respected history and criminology journals over the past few years. He has recently published *Crime and Justice 1750–1950* with Paul Lawrence, and is the editor of several books including: Godfrey, B., Emsley, C. and Dunstall, G., (eds.) *Comparative Histories of Crime* (Willan Press, 2003) and Godfrey, B. and Dunstall, G. (eds.) *Crime and Empire, 1840–1940: Criminal justice in local and global context* (Willan Press, 2005). He also has a forthcoming book in press: *The Great British Rough: Criminality and its hinterland at the fin de siècle* (Willan Press).

Mr. Cox was for several years Editor of *The Blackcountryman*, the quarterly journal of the Black Country Society, and has also written numerous articles for specialist and peer-reviewed journals, including "'A certain share of low cunning" – the provincial use and activities of Bow Street "Runners" 1792 – 1839' (*ERAS Online Journal*, Monash University, Australia) and 'The Strange Case of Eliza Price' (*Journal of the Police History Society* no. 17, 2002). He has recently had a monograph published: *The Dunsley Murder of 1812: a study in early nineteenth-century crime detection, justice and punishment* (The Dulston Press, 2003), and is currently working on a Black Country volume of the *Foul Deeds and Suspicious Deaths* series (Wharncliffe, expected 2006).

Acknowledgements

We would like to thank a number of people and organisations who have aided the writing of this book. We acknowledge the assistance of The Walker Trust who provided us with a grant; and are very grateful to Mary Mackenzie and the staff of the Shropshire Records Centre, who were all unfailingly helpful and courteous, and who directed us to documents and records of which we would otherwise have remained ignorant. We would also like to thank the magistrates and retired magistrates who allowed us to take up their precious time with interviews; and to register our appreciation of the committed volunteers at the numerous museums that we visited for the project.

The most important acknowledgement is to Catherine Trimby, Chairman of Shrewsbury Magistrates Court, who initiated our interest in this edited collection, and who has been helpful throughout the life of the project. Lastly, we would like to thank all of the people who provided chapters that we, as editors, found so pleasurable and interesting to read.

Foreword
By the Lord Lieutenant of Shropshire

The County of Shropshire has throughout the ages been well served by volunteers who have given both their time and skills to promote Local Government, Charitable Causes and, perhaps most importantly, the maintenance of Law and Order.

'*Cinderellas and Packhorses*' vividly illustrates the many diverse roles Magistrates performed within the County and it is evident too that Shropshire was amongst the most progressive in its attitude to both Prisons and Police reform.

This well researched record will certainly appeal not only to those immediately connected with the County's Magistracy but to all who appreciate a lively and entertaining account of a hitherto neglected vocation.

Algernon Heber-Percy J.P. (photograph © Derek Tamea)

Preface

From time immemorial, Justices of the Peace have been the bulwark
and personification of local justice. They feel simultaneously that
they are the Cinderellas of the judicial system and its packhorses,
handling as they do over ninety per cent of all criminal cases,
together with a great many civil ones.

Lord Phillips of Sudbury, December 2001

This edited collection of essays is the result of a collaboration between the
Walker Trust, Shropshire Archives and the Shrewsbury Magistrates Bench. The
contributors are all experts in their field, but the purpose of the book is not to be
a dry, academic tome; rather it aims to provide an informative and entertaining
insight into the history of the Shropshire Magistracy from its beginnings in the
early medieval period until the present-day.

The history of the Shropshire Magistracy is a fascinating one, about which
relatively little has been previously published. The book contains details of
the duties and responsibilities of the magistracy through history, along with
incidental details of punishments and sentences handed out to various Shropshire
miscreants throughout the centuries. There are numerous illustrations of both
personalities and buildings connected with the magistracy, and there are also
several entertaining case studies drawn from records held by Shropshire
Archives. We hope that readers will find the book informative and interesting,
and will gain as much enjoyment reading it as we did from its production.

John Speed's Map of Shropshire 1611 (© Shropshire Archives).

Speed's map illustrates Shropshire's considerable size and also demonstrates that the county was (and remains) fundamentally rural in nature, with few large centres of population

CHAPTER ONE

The English Magistracy Past and Present

The precise origins of the office of Justice of the Peace are obscure, but in essence the role evolved in England amidst the violence and turbulence of medieval feudal society. At this time, the judicial system was rooted centrally in the king, the Privy Council, Parliament, and three central courts, namely the Court of Common Pleas (which heard cases between the king's subjects), the Court of King's Bench (which involved matters of special concern to the Crown), and the Exchequer (which heard cases arising from the audit of the revenue), whose justices made regular tours of the country. In the counties and chartered boroughs the administration of justice rested largely with the Sheriff and the Coroner but in 1195 the maintenance of law and order — 'the King's peace' — was entrusted by Richard I to certain knights, the principal landowners, who commanded local respect and on whom the Crown could rely in the suppression of riots and disorders in unruly areas.[1]

The Statute of Winchester of 1285, introduced during the reign of Edward I, first defined the judicial and policing functions of these 'keepers of the peace', or *custodes pacis*, and Edward II was the first king to issue frequent commissions to *custodes pacis*, with statutes of 1308, 1316 and 1327 variously empowering them to initiate legal proceedings — to arrest people on suspicion, to deliver them to gaol, and to inquire into felonies and trespass — although they lacked the power to punish offenders. Subsequent pressures from the House of Commons, representing the interests of the gentry, for the extension of powers to these Commissions of the Peace during the Hundred Years' War with France resulted in a statute of 1361, passed during the reign of Edward III, which effectively transformed keepers into justices of the peace by authorising them to 'keep and cause to be kept all ordinances and statutes for the good of our peace' and 'to chastise and punish all persons' that offended against such ordinances and statutes, namely to try criminals accused of felonies and trespass. Moreover, in 1351, at a time of socio-economic dislocation in the aftermath of the Black Death, the Statute of Labourers provided justices with an additional responsibility, that of regulating wages and prices, an economic role which the magistracy was subsequently to develop.[2]

Thereafter, the role of the Justice of the Peace was gradually formalised and extended. A statute of 1390 provided that each county should appoint eight justices, although more were duly appointed in the most populous counties, whilst the qualification to be a Justice of the Peace was determined by statutes of 1389, 1414 and 1439, which nominally required them to be drawn from the 'most sufficient knights, esquires and gentleman of the law' resident within each county and possessing a freehold estate of not less than £20 per annum (this remained the essential qualification until 1732, when it was revised and upgraded to an estate in land worth £100 per annum, clear of incumbrances). The office of magistrate was essentially voluntary and unpaid; although statutes of 1388 and 1390 entitled all magistrates who were not peers of the realm to receive wages of 4s. a day for their attendance at the Quarter Sessions, up to a maximum of twelve days a year. In practice, their appointment was subject to local influences and the social composition of the Commission of the Peace (the corporate body of Justices) was characterised by class-exclusiveness in both countryside (where the gentry predominated, almost as if by hereditary right) and the towns (where merchants and lawyers predominated). These men of property were also, frequently, Members of Parliament.[3] Nevertheless, the Justices of the Peace were part of their local community and by the late Middle Ages, with their increasingly wide range of judicial and civil responsibilities, they constituted the best means of organising local government in England. Their role in imposing the law on the local level was crucial, since it was the magistrates' duty, once an allegation of law-breaking had been made, to take evidence from the aggrieved party and from witnesses, to take a statement from the accused, and to decide whether, as a misdemeanour, the case could be dealt with summarily or, as a more serious offence, it should be advanced to a higher court. In this latter context, it was the J.P.s' responsibility to bail or remand in custody the accused, ensure that the defendant, plaintiff and witnesses attended the court, and ensure that all appropriate documentation be collated and presented during the court proceedings.[4]

The magistracy continued to evolve during the Tudor and Stuart periods, despite the political and religious dislocations that accompanied the Reformation, the Civil War, the Cromwellian interregnum, and the Restoration. By 1580 there were some 1,738 J.P.s scattered throughout the counties of England and Wales. By an Act of 1590 the procedures for appointing justices were reformulated, emphasising the judicial nature of the office by requiring justices to enforce peace-keeping statutes and inquiring by jury into specific offences. On his appointment, the magistrate took the oath of office and the oaths of supremacy and allegiance. Thereafter, he was effectively a magistrate for life. Magistrates were expected to act in various ways according to the business in hand: severally as individuals sitting alone; jointly with one or more magistrates in a particular Division; and collectively as a General Sessions of the whole county, a public assembly where the Sheriff provided a court of justice.[5]

Whilst the most serious felonies (offences warranting the death penalty) were dealt with at the Assizes, which met twice a year — at Lent and Trinity — in each county, presided over by a Circuit Judge, the General Sessions, to which all county magistrates were summoned, comprised the first stage of the criminal process and met four times a year — at Hilary, Easter, Midsummer and Michaelmas — and eventually became popularly known as the Court of Quarter Sessions. These were normally, but not exclusively held in county towns. Meeting variously at the local castle, or cathedral chapter-house, or even tavern, the Quarter Sessions constituted the supreme county authority, for in addition to criminal jurisdiction, its responsibilities also encompassed the civil administration of the county, including the maintenance of bridges, gaols and Houses of Correction, the regulation of wages, prices and rates of land carriage, the imposition of special levies for parish needs, the suppression of disorderly houses, and the appointment of parish constables.[6] Moreover, during the Reformation, magistrates were given the additional responsibility of tracing and prosecuting recusants, although in predominantly Roman Catholic counties such as Lancashire some sympathetic local magistrates ignored this charge.[7]

Magistrates were also directed by various statutes and Privy Council orders to group themselves by local Divisions and to assemble each month at what became known as Special Sessions, attended by local Hundred and parish officers. The judicial powers of these Divisional Sessions, sometimes referred to as 'Justices' Assemblies', encompassed all offences against the peace, other than the actual trial of offences requiring a Jury, hence magistrates could try, convict and punish persons guilty of minor offences and also hear and commit for trial at the Quarter Sessions those accused of assault, larceny and graver offences such as murder. At these Divisional Sessions, magistrates could, for example, fine or commit to prison persons participating in riots or forcible entry, unlicensed ale-house keepers who supplied drink, servants leaving their employment before the expiry of their term, any woman between the ages of twelve and forty deemed to be living idly and refusing to be put in service, and any person killing game or taking eggs. Magistrates were also responsible, from 1552, for the licensing of alehouses, which, from 1729, were granted at a special meeting of the magistrates each September (the 'Brewster Sessions'). Moreover, in consequence of legislation introduced in 1536, 1559, 1572, 1598 and 1601 under the auspices of the Elizabethan Poor Law, magistrates were required to form county divisions for dealing with vagrancy, poor relief, and various offences, and two or more magistrates were required to meet annually in each locality in order to appoint the Overseers of the Poor for each parish, to audit their accounts, to sanction the Poor Rate, to order the maintenance of a bastard child by its alleged father, and, from 1662, to make orders for the removal of paupers to their place of settlement. In time, these local meetings of the magistracy developed into the 'Privy' or 'Petty' Sessions, held initially in the village inn, or even at the home of a magistrate, where a range of civil and judicial business was transacted by a minimum of two magistrates.[8]

The individual magistrate also held considerable power. He could, for example, issues summonses requiring persons to appear at the forthcoming Sessions; order by warrant the arrest and safe custody of a suspected offender; order suspected persons to find sureties for good behaviour, on pain of imprisonment; and summarily commit any person obstructing the course of justice by contempt of court. He could also, without corroboration, variously fine, place in the stocks, or imprison any person who, in his view, had uttered a profane oath, was evidently drunk, and had either attended 'blood-sports' or pursued his employment on a Sunday. His greatest discretion, however, lay with the vague offence of vagrancy. Here, and subject to evidence from the parish constable or another witness, the magistrate could summarily convict a person of any act of vagrancy, punish them in the stocks or pillory, or with a public whipping, and return them to their place of settlement.[9]

Neither was the authority of the magistracy limited to county matters. During the medieval period over two hundred towns achieved borough status through the granting of Royal or Seigniorial Charters of Incorporation and established

Moveable stocks, Much Wenlock Guildhall

their own Quarter and Sessions independent of county jurisdiction. Normally, the Borough Bench comprised the leading municipal officials such as the mayor, aldermen, recorder and bailiff who, by occupation, were largely men of trade and commerce, with representatives of the major local industries. This local oligarchy was entrusted not only with the maintenance of law and order within a relatively small geographical area within their jurisdiction, appointing constables, watchmen, street-keepers and gaolers, but also with the administration of a range of borough matters.[10]

Yet in practice the magistrate was also the arbiter of two contemporary concepts of order. On the one hand, there was the centralised notion of order as embodied in the statutes issued by Tudor and Stuart parliaments which magistrates were expected to uphold. These co-existed, on the other hand, with the norms and attitudes that governed social behaviour in the local community (of which the magistrate was also a member), and there is evidence to suggest that parochial officials were often reluctant to bring before the magistrates offenders other than those who, by their actions, had stepped beyond the 'moral community' by putting at risk the greater part of the community.[11]

It has been estimated that by 1689, the year of the 'Glorious Revolution', around eighty Commissions of the Peace were in operation in the counties of England and Wales, with a collective complement of some 3,000 magistrates. Indeed, the Justices of the Peace had effectively become the rulers of the county, the symbols of local government, exercising, judicially and administratively, the many statutes relating to police and social economy,[12] and throughout the 18th century, with their considerable discretionary powers,[13] they felt at liberty to administer local affairs as they thought fit, whether as isolated individuals, acting on their own initiative, or collectively through Petty, Special and Quarter Sessions.

The distribution of magistrates throughout the country, with the exception of the Corporate Boroughs, at the start of the 18th century is uncertain. As the Webbs observed, 'an active Justice of the Peace grew, could not be made, and was not always to be found', noting the differentiation between magistrates in terms of their social background, practices and ability.[14] In some counties, including Devonshire, Gloucestershire and Middlesex, men of good estates and ancient families were disqualified or dropped from the Commission of the Peace due to their political or religious views in the aftermath of the English Revolution. They were replaced by men of humbler station – 'the Justices of Mean Degree' – who were often barely qualified for the role. Then there were the 'Trading Justices', men who intrigued themselves into some Commissions for pecuniary gain by charging fees for every act that was performed.[15] In Middlesex and Surrey, such corrupt practices gave rise within the Metropolitan district to the emergence of the 'Court Justice', a magistrate to whom the government gave instructions and on whom it could rely during an emergency, including riots and disorders, in the capital. The most famous of these magistrates was Sir Thomas de Veil, who held the post from 1729 to 1747. De Veil received a Treasury grant of £250 a year for his services and operated from an office in Bow Street, Covent Garden.[16] Subsequently, during the magistracies of Henry Fielding (from 1748–1754) and his brother, John Fielding (from 1754–1780), the Bow Street Police Office became the centre of police administration in London where, from 1792, paid 'Stipendiary' or 'Police' magistrates were appointed for the summary courts.[17] In the rural counties, the magistracy was often sparsely distributed, allowing some men to wield enormous power at the local level. Described by the Webbs as 'Rural Tyrants',[18] these magistrates were satirised in the novels of Tobias Smollett[19] and Henry Fielding,[20] although such stereotypes were probably unrepresentative of the whole, for most country gentlemen who dominated the magistracy had been well educated at grammar or public school and, occasionally, university.[21] Moreover, during the 18th century, shortages of suitably qualified magistrates in some districts led to the admission of Anglican clergymen into the Commission of the Peace. These 'Clerical Justices' were, as owners of glebe and tithe, freeholders and they generally possessed a greater knowledge of English law than was the norm amongst the magistracy. In some counties, notably Cambridge, Hereford, Cornwall, Lincoln, Somerset and Norfolk, clergymen comprised more than half of the acting magistrates, and they also proved to be particularly diligent, often chairing the Quarter Sessions.[22] In 1832, the year of the Great Reform Act, there were 5,371 county magistrates, of whom 1,354 were clergymen.[23]

By the early 19th century, the function of keeping the peace formed only part of the responsibilities of the magistrate, who was effectively 'judge, prosecutor, administrator, policeman, welfare officer, auditor and supervisor of all that went on in the countryside'.[24] Indeed, the magistrates' administrative duties at the Quarter Sessions had increased substantially. Their chief business lay with the administration of the county rate, the total cost of which increased in England and Wales from £315,000 to £783,000 between 1792 and 1832.[25] Magistrates were also responsible, from 1792, for the regulation of Turnpike Trusts. Yet they also acquired additional responsibilities in regard to social administration as a result of the growing humanitarian movement of the period.[26] In 1802 magistrates were required to enforce legislation in regard to the employment of pauper apprentices in the newly-emerging cotton mills of Lancashire and in 1808 they were authorised to build county lunatic asylums for the proper care of pauper and criminal lunatics, to pay for this from a special rate, and to supervise the subsequent administration of the asylum (a role they exercised for much of the 19th century).[27] Moreover, the Gaols Act of 1823, which provided the basis of a reformed prison system, required magistrates to appoint Visiting

Committees and to submit quarterly returns to the Quarter Sessions and then to the Home Office.[28]

In essence, however, the magistracy represented property and this placed them in an ambivalent position in regard to the population as a whole because whilst they embodied the traditions of a hierarchical and paternalist society in their social and administrative roles as the protectors of the poor, variously administering poor law legislation, regulating wages and prosecuting forestalling (a practice which led to high bread prices and popular distress), as landowners they increasingly saw their own economic interests and prosperity best served by market forces (*laissez-faire*) rather than by regulation. Hence they upheld and enforced – often summarily in their own homes — the Game Laws, a long-standing focus for rural discontent, and the Combination Acts, a focus for radical agitation in urban-industrial districts.[29]

Tensions between the magistracy and the labouring poor of town and country were made more transparent during the early 19th century, at a time of acute social and economic change in consequence of the agricultural and industrial revolutions, when the magistracy was confronted by the problem of working-class urban and rural protest. The prime role of the magistracy was to maintain public order and to punish crime and, in the absence of a professional police force, it was the responsibility of the magistrate, when riot and disorder threatened, to read the Riot Act, to swear in special constables and, if necessary, to summon the military in order to restore order. In the countryside, magistrates played a key role in the suppression of a range of local disturbances, including food riots, anti-enclosure riots and anti-turnpike riots, and more widespread regional disorders such as the 'Bread or Blood' disturbances in East Anglia in 1816 and, later, the 'Swing Riots' of 1830–31 in southern England. Likewise, in the industrial districts of the North and the Midlands, they had to contend with the threat to public order posed by Luddism in 1811–12, radical agitation in the immediate post-Napoleonic War period (culminating in the infamous 'Peterloo Massacre' in Manchester in 1819) and, later, Chartism.[30]

Moreover, with accelerated urbanisation and industrialisation, contemporary fears abounded that crime, and particularly serious crime, was on the increase. Indeed, quantitatively if not qualitatively, the levels of recorded crime do suggest a marked increase during this period and, by mid-century, more criminal acts were being brought to light by reformed provincial police forces and prosecuted in the courts, which entailed more work for the magistracy in their judicial roles. This burden was exacerbated by the progressive extension of state legislation in regard to summary jurisdiction, which transferred the jurisdiction of a range of offences, once deemed serious, from the Assizes to the Quarter Sessions and Petty Sessions in order to make the prosecution of such offences more speedy and efficient. For example, in 1828 common assault was defined as a summary offence; in 1847 and 1850 the Juvenile Offenders Acts made simple larcenies committed by children under the ages of 14 and 16 summary offences; in 1853 the principle was extended to aggravated assaults on women and children; in 1855 the Criminal Justice Act transferred larceny cases under the value of 5s. to summary jurisdiction; in 1879 the Summary Jurisdiction Act extended summary justice to all children under the age of 12 for all offences, other than murder and manslaughter, to juveniles under the age of 16 for larceny, embezzlement and receiving stolen goods, and to all adults charged with larceny under the value of £2, provided they pleaded guilty. Thus, whilst the Assizes continued to deal with the most serious crimes such as murder, manslaughter, rape, burglary, robbery with violence and arson, in the Quarter and Petty Sessions, particularly in the boroughs, the magistracy was overwhelmed by a bewildering array of less-serious offences, ranging from assault, affray, drunk and disorderly behaviour, petty theft and vagrancy to breaches of a host of local by-laws.[31]

By contrast, the administrative duties of the magistracy were modified during the 19th century by increasing state intervention in social policy. The 1830s and 1840s witnessed the introduction of Benthamite-inspired legislation designed to provide a centralised blueprint for addressing contemporary social problems. The 1833 Factory Act, the 1834 Poor Law Amendment Act, the 1835 Prisons Act and the 1848 Public Health Act all represented statutory responses to the findings of Royal Commissions and Select Committees of Parliament, and in each case they not only established centralised agencies in London to administer the new systems but also instituted the principle of government inspection in order to ensure that the localities complied with the new legislation. Although this 'revolution in government' was gradual and often permissive in nature, it marked a breach with the traditions of 'laissez-faire' and challenged the autonomy of local communities in administering their own affairs. Indeed, in the provinces, there was both distrust of and distaste for intrusive centralising tendencies and the magistracy, in many ways the symbol of localism, often found itself at the forefront of opposition to state intervention in social policy. In the north of England, for example, some local J.P.s played a prominent role in the anti-Poor Law movement, which rendered the abolition of outdoor relief (as envisaged in the 1834 Act) a dead letter, whilst also blunting the effective implementation of factory legislation during the 1840s and contributing to the more widespread opposition to the Public Health Act of 1848.[32]

State intervention also encompassed police reform, which was progressively addressed by the Metropolitan Police Act of 1829, which established the 'New Police' in London; the Municipal Corporations Act of 1835, which required the municipal boroughs to establish reformed forces under the direction of a Watch Committee (drawn from elected councillors); the County Police Act of 1839, which allowed the magistrates in Quarter Sessions to form county police forces in all or part of the county jurisdiction; and the County and Borough Police Act of 1856, which made the establishment of county and borough police forces mandatory and established Her Majesty's Inspectorate (HMI) of Constabulary, who duly inspected 239 county and borough forces (finding 120 of them to be 'inefficient').[33] Although the process of reform was gradual and piecemeal, by the 1860s the traditional patchwork of local police-keeping mechanisms rooted in the J.P., the parish constable, day and night watches, and private associations for the prosecution of felons had been replaced by increasingly professional and publicly accepted provincial police forces. Although the provincial magistracy held an intrinsic commitment to the maintenance of law and order and to the prevention, detection and punishment of crime, their response to these developments, which appeared to both undermine their traditional law-enforcement roles and challenge the concept of local control of policing, was often lukewarm.[34] The permissive County Police Act of 1839 aroused considerable opposition from some county J.P.s, and the Act was only adopted, either wholly or in part (and especially in populous and industrial districts), in 35 of the 57 counties of England and Wales. Elsewhere, the parish constable system was upheld by the county J.P.s until 1856. Indeed, in 1829 the Cheshire magistrates secured a private Act of Parliament — the Cheshire Constabulary Act — which enabled them to establish and control their own county force until 1856, when they were forced to comply with the County and Borough Police Act.[35]

The reform and democratisation of local government during the 19th century also had profound consequences for the magistracy. Following in the wake of parliamentary reform in 1832, the Municipal Corporations Act of 1835 reformed the government of 178 chartered boroughs by replacing the old municipal corporations with town councils elected on the basis of household suffrage, with a three-year residential and rate-paying qualification. Thereafter, incorporation became a test of municipal identity and many industrial and manufacturing towns previously denied borough status and administered by county authorities sought and acquired Charters of Incorporation, including Birmingham, Bradford, Leeds and Manchester, and by the end of the century there were over 300 municipal boroughs.[36] In consequence of the 1835 Act, the office of magistrate was severed from corporate office (although the mayor remained a J.P. *ex officio*) and borough magistrates were appointed, like their counterparts in the counties, by the Lord Chancellor. The Act also separated judicial and administrative functions, for the bulk of the administrative work previously undertaken by the Borough Bench was transferred to the new town councils. Borough councils were also allowed to appoint Stipendiary magistrates if they so wished, subject to the approval of the Home Secretary.[37] The reform of county government proceeded at a slower pace, but the County Councils Act of 1888 established 62 county councils and 49 county borough councils. These elected bodies subsequently took over much of the administrative work previously undertaken by the county magistracy in Quarter Sessions, although in the elections held in the immediate aftermath of the Act it was noted that many of the county councillors and alderman who were elected had previously been county magistrates.[38]

The social composition and social standing of the magistracy also changed during the period. In the counties, where the Bench was the preserve of the landed classes, the social composition of the magistracy was recast by the gradual assimilation of middle-class Justices into its ranks. Although some Lord Lieutenants (who advised the Lord Chancellor on the appointment of magistrates) and the country gentry were initially reluctant to admit 'men of trade' to the Bench, this was often tempered in practice by the need to maintain law and order in the rapidly-expanding industrial districts of South Lancashire, the West Riding of Yorkshire, South Wales and the Black Country, where many industrial towns had yet to secure charters of incorporation and where the number of active magistrates was in short supply. For example, in Staffordshire, Earl Talbot, the Lord Lieutenant from 1812 to 1849, was determined to preserve the political and social dominance of the Tory nobility and gentry in the county and regarded persons connected with industry and commerce, including local coal and iron masters, as socially unfit for appointment to the Bench.[39] However, Chartist disorders in the Black Country between 1839 and 1842, which exposed the shortage of active magistrates in the region and pointed to the need for the support of local manufacturers in face of radical working-class protest, ultimately forced Talbot to relent. Thereafter, local manufacturers were admitted to the County Bench, a policy continued by subsequent Lord Lieutenants.[40] Indeed, it has been suggested that by thus gratifying the social and political aspirations of middle-class manufacturers, the landed classes were not only responding realistically to changing social conditions but were also subtly maintaining the established order of social relationships by merely expanding the circle of landed allies on the county Bench.[41] Moreover, the acquisition of borough status by many industrial towns after 1835 also witnessed the appointment of factory owners, iron-masters, manufacturers and men of commerce and the professions to the local Bench, although there is some evidence to suggest that such men did not always administer the law impartially. In Wolverhampton, iron-master J.P.s favoured the side of the masters during industrial disputes and displayed a reluctance to uphold the Truck Acts (in which some of them held an interest),[42] whilst in the West Riding of Yorkshire mill-owning magistrates were particularly zealous in prosecuting and punishing workers in the woollen mills for theft from the workplace.[43] Nevertheless, by the end of the century, both the county and borough magistracy was far less socially exclusive and represented a much broader range of local interests than before, thereby reflecting broader changes in society as a whole.

This process continued during the 20th century. In 1906 the property qualification for J.P.s was abolished. In 1910 the Royal Commission on the Appointment of Justices of the Peace recommended that appointments to the Bench should be opened up to people of all social classes, irrespective of their political and religious beliefs and, following a successful experiment in Devon in 1907, many counties began to establish committees to advise the Lord Lieutenant on the appointment of magistrates. In 1925 membership of these advisory committees was restricted to a period of six years, rather than for life, with members retiring every three years in rotation, in order to ensure that members were drawn from all sections of the community. In 1919 the Sex Disqualification (Removal) Act enabled women to be admitted to the Bench. The first female magistrate, Ada Summers,

the Mayor of Stalybridge, was sworn in on 31st December 1919 and in the following five years no fewer than 1,200 women were appointed as J.P.s. The first female magistrate in Shropshire was Mrs. Marion Cock, appointed in 1929. Currently almost half of the 30,000 lay (unpaid) magistrates in England and Wales are women.

Moreover, the magistracy was progressively professionalised during the 20th century, in part as a result of the extension of summary jurisdiction. In particular, the establishment of specialised juvenile courts (which have a civil and criminal jurisdiction) under the terms of the 1908 'Children's Charter' and the 1933 Children's and Young Persons Act, have required the appointment of magistrates with specialised qualifications for adjudicated in such cases and have entailed an increasing amount of work for the Bench. In 1948 the Royal Commission on Justices of the Peace recommended that magistrates should receive

Marion Wallace Cock,
first female magistrate in Shropshire
and mayor of Shrewsbury 1934/5
(© Shropshire Archives, PH/S/13/M/11)

appropriate training and a compulsory training scheme was finally introduced in 1966 which, by requiring new magistrates to complete a specialist course (covering court procedure, criminal legislation, and sentencing powers and options) within twelve months of their appointment, heralded the demise of the traditional role of the J.P. as an untrained amateur. There are no longer any formal or legal qualifications to become a magistrate, although they must be between the ages of 18 and 70 (when they must retire) and applicants are expected to possess intelligence, common sense and impartiality. Approximately 1,600 magistrates are appointed to the Bench each year and they are expected to attend an average of 35 and a minimum of 26 half-day sittings at the magistrates' court per annum. They continue to be unpaid, although they do receive subsistence and travel expenses.[44]

There are currently over 700 magistrates' courts in England and Wales and they handle summarily approximately 97% of all criminal cases. In 2004 alone, more than 1,500,000 cases were dealt with by the magistracy, within which motoring offences and various breaches of the peace loomed large. Unlike its medieval and early modern predecessors, however, the modern magistracy can only impose a maximum penalty of six months' imprisonment for such offences, although it can impose fines of up to £5,000 for each offence. Other penalties such as community orders, including supervision by a Probation Officer, and unpaid work, drug or alcohol treatment requirements are also available. More serious indictable offences have, since the Courts Act of 1971, been advanced to trial by jury at the Crown Court, which replaced the jurisdiction of the Assizes and Quarter Sessions.[45]

The judicial and administrative responsibilities of the provincial magistracy in England and Wales have been transformed during the past eight hundred years. During this period, the magistracy has been required to respond and adapt to broader shifts in the social, economic, political and cultural fabric of society. Yet there have also been continuities within this evolutionary process and, at the dawn of the 21st century, the Justice of the Peace continues to fulfil the essential role of 'keeper of the peace' within the local community, as this unique study of the history of the Shropshire Magistracy illustrates.

CHAPTER TWO

Shropshire Justices of the Peace before the 18th century

Until the late 13th century Shropshire (like most if not all other counties of England) lacked an organized system for bringing offenders to justice. There were ancient local courts for each hundred (an administrative sub-division of a county, which had it own fiscal, military and judicial functions and responsibilities) and the king's own justices visited the county from time to time in order to try the most serious offences. The king's own justices were senior Westminster judges who from 1166 were sent out on regular occasions to hear cases in regional circuits. For example, a court sat at Shrewsbury from Friday 14 January 1256 to Wednesday 16 February, hearing 482 civil cases and 428 criminal cases.[1] From the middle of the 13th century, more serious cases came to be heard by Assize judges, senior judges appointed by the king, who rode the Assize circuits of England twice a year, dealing with cases that were deemed beyond the capability or jurisdiction of local justices of the peace.

However, none of the various courts could operate effectively without a police system to bring wrongdoers before them. The sheriff had a small number of officers at his command and holders of large estates sometimes had private police forces, but it was often left to villages and townships to police themselves and to catch offenders if they could. This was a communal system of policing at its most basic, dating back to Anglo-Saxon times. Known as 'Hue and Cry', the system required that all members of a neighbourhood should be responsible for pursuing and capturing suspected criminals. The system was formally strengthened by the Statute of Winchester of 1285 which stated that:

> Cries shall be solemnly made in all Counties, Hundreds, Markets, Fairs and all other place where great resort of people is, so that none shall excuse himself by ignorance, that from henceforth every County be so well kept, that immediately, upon such robberies and felonies committed, fresh suit shall be made from town to town.

The system continued in statute (if not in practice) until 1827.

In 1285 the government also tried to introduce throughout the country a system of constables elected by each neighbourhood, who would police that area. It was the beginning of the office of petty (sometimes called 'parish') constable, which survived until the mid 19th century. These petty constables were elected yearly and were unpaid apart from fees and expenses. Many were therefore inefficient and less than keen to pursue suspects in the same community in which they lived, often fearing verbal opprobrium or even physical violence from neighbours. Recent research has somewhat modified the view of all petty constables as inept and worthless fellows in the mould of Shakespeare's comic creations of Dogberry and Verges in *Much Ado About Nothing* (and it must be remembered that these two bumbling inepts did in fact get their man), but the policing situation throughout the medieval and early modern period remained far from perfect or professional. Shropshire's first professional police forces did not appear until 1836, when Borough forces at Ludlow, Bridgnorth, Oswestry and Shrewsbury were sworn in, while a County Police force did not come into existence until 1839.[2]

In 1287 a pair of county landholders was appointed by the king in each shire to supervise the constables' conduct. These two, called 'keepers of the peace', were the forerunners of the justices of the peace who were to assume the dominant role in county government in the later Middle Ages. In Shropshire the first two keepers were John FitzEyre and William of Hodnet, but it took a long time for the new scheme to gain acceptance in the county. Although an improvement on the old locally-devised police measures, it marked an increase in government intervention in Shropshire's affairs and placed an unwelcome new obligation on each community. Continuously from 1368 the keepers of the peace were allowed by the king to sentence minor offenders brought before them. Thenceforth they were invariably called 'justices' of the peace, and by the later Middle Ages had supplanted the hundred courts in dealing with all minor offences except the most trivial. The most serious crimes remained the province of the visiting royal justices.

The commission of the peace
The names of the J.P.s appointed were listed in a royal document issued for the county, called a 'commission of the peace', which was re-issued whenever a name was to be added or removed. Soon it became a matter of local prestige to appear in the peace commission, and remained so until modern times. In practice the appointments were not made by the king personally but by his ministers, usually on the recommendation of an influential person in the county (eventually on that of the Lord Lieutenant). Thus the peace commission could be manipulated by a local nobleman in order to enhance his local influence,

or by the government of the day to enhance its own security. This began to happen in Shropshire in the later 14th century, and continued until the early 18th century. There was also a tendency for the commission to increase in size: in the 14th century the Shropshire commission comprised no more than about six men, but by 1608 there were 54.

In the 1390s the Shropshire J.P.s were mostly friends or relatives of Richard FitzAlan, 6th earl of Arundel, the county's leading nobleman. His ancestors had been Sheriffs of Shropshire 1155–1201. In 1397 he was executed for treason (after incurring the displeasure of Richard II by opposing many of the king's favourites) and his followers were dismissed from the Shropshire commission, to be replaced by friends of the king. On Henry IV's accession in 1399 the former king's friends were dropped and supporters of the new earl, Thomas FitzAlan, were put on. When Thomas died childless in 1415 the predominant influence in Shropshire passed to John Talbot, Lord Furnivalle, who became earl of Shrewsbury in 1442 and died in 1453. He and his son, both Lancastrians in the Wars of the Roses, established and maintained their influence over membership of the Shropshire commission, whose composition was thus mainly Lancastrian until 1460. In that year the second earl was killed at the battle of Northampton, and from that time more Yorkists were included.

After the battle of Bosworth and Henry VII's accession (1485) many of Shropshire's Yorkist J.P.s were removed, to be replaced by Henry's supporters. In 1493 the prince of Wales's council was granted additional powers so that it came to have a civil and criminal jurisdiction not only over Wales but also over Shropshire, Herefordshire, Worcestershire, and Gloucestershire. It was composed of the leading lawyers and landholders of its constituent area. Its head was called the president (or lord president) and its headquarters was Ludlow castle. In the 16th century many council members were added to the peace commissions of the constituent counties, at times outnumbering the local men, but these outsiders rarely attended Quarter Sessions and there was usually little council interference in Shropshire government. An exceptional period was the presidency (1534–43) of Rowland Lee, bishop of Coventry and Lichfield. He waged a successful campaign of terror against lawbreakers in Wales and the border counties, and used county Quarter Sessions, reinforced with council members, as a means of sentencing large numbers of them to death. There was little political alteration to the Shropshire commission during the religious changes under Edward VI (1547–53) and Mary I (1553–8), though Mary did appoint Edmund Plowden, a notable Roman Catholic, and dropped Sir George Blount, who had supported the attempt to put Lady Jane Grey on the throne. Elizabeth I's establishment of the Church of England resulted in a number of dismissals of Roman Catholics and their sympathizers from the Shropshire bench early in her reign. By the 1590s appointments of Shropshire J.P.s were being influenced by the queen's favourite, the earl of Essex, and in 1601, when Essex was executed for treason, his local supporter Sir Henry Bromley was quickly dropped from the Shropshire commission.

The local-government policy that had evolved in England, that of rule by the chief landholders of each county, especially as justices of the peace, underwent its severest test in the 17th century, and emerged with great credit. Shropshire's inhabitants felt powerfully attached to their traditional leaders, some of whom, like the Corbets, the Leightons, and the Newports, had been in county government for generations. Some 17th-century governments tried to ignore these traditional loyalties and to impose county leaders of humbler background or revolutionary ideas. The experiments simply did not work. Until the 1640s the Shropshire magistracy was overwhelmingly conservative and royalist. Charles I, however, came under increasing pressure from a critical Parliament, and had to take note of Parliament's views because he could not levy adequate taxes without its consent. Thus in 1625 Parliament forced him to dismiss suspected Roman Catholics and their sympathizers from the county benches: 22 were removed in Shropshire. In the late 1630s, as a direct confrontation with Parliament became increasingly likely, Charles began to fill up the Shropshire commission with men he supposed friendly, but by 1641 he was being forced by Parliament to appoint its own supporters in Shropshire, such as William Pierrepont, Thomas Mytton, and Humphrey Mackworth.

Civil war broke out in 1642 and in 1644 appointments of Shropshire J.P.s fell wholly under Parliament's control. The royalist J.P.s were all dropped, but Parliament's appointees were moderate men, not far removed in social position from their predecessors. In the late 1640s, however, extremists took control of central government. They beheaded the king in 1649 and purged the county commissions of moderates. Until 1653 the Shropshire commission thus consisted mainly of tradesmen and farmers, who had radical views but no following in the county at large. During Cromwell's time as Lord Protector (1653–8) it was necessary, for effective local government, to restore moderates to the Shropshire bench. They soon came to predominate, and were ready by 1660 to accept Charles II's restoration. They had nevertheless acted disloyally to the Crown; all, with the possible exception of Job Charlton, were dismissed, though some were reinstated within a few years. Charles's new Shropshire commission was fiercely loyal to the king and the Church of England. The county's ruling class was fully restored.

By the late 1670s, however, political divisions were beginning to appear in the Shropshire commission, particularly over whether Charles II's brother James, a Roman Catholic, should eventually succeed him. Those who wanted James excluded from the succession were called Exclusionists or Whigs, and in the early 1680s Charles systematically removed them from the magistracy; some 21 were dropped in Shropshire. When James II succeeded in 1685 the

Shropshire bench was thus solidly Tory, and loyal to him personally though not to his religion. Soon, however, James turned the J.P.s vehemently against him by trying to grant toleration to the public practice of Catholicism and to restore Roman Catholics to official positions in central and local government. In 1687 he added nine Catholics to the Shropshire commission, and in 1688 replaced three-quarters of the Shropshire J.P.s when they refused to accept his pro-Catholic policies. He tried these tactics in all counties, with results disastrous for himself. In Shropshire, as all over the country, local government broke down and riotous mobs took to the streets. James had to flee the country and William and Mary were invited to accept the Crown. The dismissed Tory J.P.s were restored in Shropshire, and for 20 years the bench comprised an uneasy mixture of the parties. After the Tory victory in the 1710 general election 39 men, nearly all Tories, were added immediately to the Shropshire commission, and 19 more by 1714. In 1712 Eldred Lancelot Lee, an obscure and unpopular local J.P., whose one advantage was a family connexion with Lord Keeper Harcourt (the minister responsible for appointing J.P.s), secured the dismissal of seven Whigs from the Shropshire bench. In 1714, however, the Whigs won the general election; many Shropshire Whigs were added or brought back to the commission and 15 Tories were removed. The result was an even balance of the parties.

The J.P.s were not necessarily less efficient for being appointed on political grounds, for their duties were not of a political character. In any case their efficiency was continually watched by the Privy Council and the assize justices. Moreover the successive political upheavals give a false impression of discontinuity. From the 14th century onwards some members of the Shropshire bench were recognized by the others as their leaders. Often they were experienced lawyers whose knowledge was too valuable to be lost by political purges. One such was Thomas Horde of Bridgnorth, who remained the leading Shropshire J.P. throughout the troubled period from 1458 to 1498, with scarcely a break. By 1608, of the 54 J.P.s, only an average of 12 attended Quarter Sessions; these were the only J.P.s whose views really mattered, and these were the ones who were often left untouched by the political changes in the commission. In the 17th century changing governments engineered sweeping alterations in the peace commission as a whole, but hesitated to interfere with the leaders of Quarter Sessions, those cautious and moderate J.P.s whose outlook and experience gave them the predominant influence locally. Thus, even during the Interregnum (1649–60), the conduct of Quarter-Sessions business went on much as before; it was little affected by national politics.

Quarter Sessions
From 1362 the keepers (later justices) of the peace were required by statute to hold sessions every quarter. The requirement remained until Quarter Sessions

were abolished in 1971 (being replaced by the present system of magistrates' courts, crown courts and county courts). When central government was weak, however, the 1362 statute was not enforced, and it was not until the later 15th century that the sessions in Shropshire were regularly held. Before that there were sometimes only two sessions a year, and in some especially bad periods none at all. Before the mid-16th century the sessions were held at various Shropshire towns, probably according to the preference of the leading J.P., but thenceforth they always met at Shrewsbury, almost certainly (until 1712) at the castle.

One case heard at the Quarter Sessions in late April 1583, illustrates the often immediate and corporeal forms of punishment that magistrates could mete out to miscreants. James Lloyd, the servant of an eminent public figure, was brought before the magistrates charged with forging his master's writing.

Lloyd was employed by Sir Henry Sidney (1529–86), who was Lord President of the Council in the Marches 1559–86 and was responsible for rebuilding parts of Ludlow Castle, including the Judge's Lodgings (completed in 1581).

Sir Henry Sidney had been a childhood companion of King Edward VI (who had reputedly died in his arms), and had remained an important personage during the reign of Elizabeth. Although the family seat was at Penshurst in Kent, Sir Henry had many connections with Shropshire and his son Philip was educated at Shrewsbury School. By 1583 Sir Henry seems to have been in somewhat straitened circumstances despite Philip's arranged marriage to Sir Francis Walsingham's daughter. A letter written by Sir Henry to Sir Francis on

Ludlow castle, showing the Great Tower (centre-left)
and the Judges' Lodgings (centre-right),
with Sir Henry Sidney's coat of arms above the entrance gate

1st March 1583 describes himself as 'having not so much grain as will feed a mutton', as being 'toothless and trembling' and '£5,000 in debt'.[3]

It is not recorded what documents were falsely signed by James Lloyd, but the very fact that he could write suggests that he was a personal aide of Sir Henry's rather than a general domestic servant. He would have done well to heed the words written by Sir Henry to his son Philip in 1555/6, when he exhorted the young man to 'be humble and obedient to your masters, for unless you frame yourself to obey others, yea, and feel in yourself what obedience is, you shall never be able to tell others to obey you'.[4]

Lloyd's sentence was immediate and harsh; he was taken to the pillory that stood in Shrewsbury's Market Square, and one of his ears was nailed to the board before he was publicly whipped — his attempts to dodge the whip presumably adding to his already considerable discomfort. Such physical punishments continued to be widespread until the early 19th century — there are numerous recorded cases of felons being sentenced by Quarter Sessions magistrates to be burnt on the hand as late as the 1770s.

Until the late 16th century each Quarter Sessions usually lasted only one day; by the 1590s, however, as the J.P.s' duties increased, sessions of two or three days became normal in Shropshire. Sessions lasted two or three days in the 17th century and attendances fluctuated between about 12 and 20. In 1712 the Whig lord-lieutenant, Lord Bradford, whose family had owned Shrewsbury castle since the 1660s, was dismissed by the Tory government, and at about the same time several Whigs were dismissed from the peace commission. Bradford

Shrewsbury castle, site of Shropshire Quarter Sessions until 1712

19

could not tolerate the continued use of his property by a Tory-dominated Quarter Sessions, and so from 1712 sessions had to be held at the Shrewsbury guildhall instead, by agreement with the corporation. This was the beginning of an increasingly abrasive accommodation-sharing partnership between county and borough, which was not resolved until 1915.

The earliest known clerk to the Shropshire Quarter Sessions, the 'clerk of the peace', was Richard Oteley, who is first mentioned in 1391. The office continued in existence until 1971. The clerk was usually appointed by the leading J.P. of the day, himself described in the peace commission as the *custos rotulorum* or 'keeper of the rolls' (i.e. the records of Quarter Sessions). Until at least the 18th century the *custos*, as a matter of course, appointed someone to whom he owed a favour, as a friend, relative, or employee. Until modern times this was the usual way of filling all non-elective posts in central and local government; the choice of a friend did not imply that the appointee would be incompetent, any more than the modern method of open competition among strangers implies the opposite. The Shropshire clerks were usually local attorneys and thus reasonably well qualified to deal with the written work of sessions and to look after the records. From 1631 the office of *custos rotulorum* in Shropshire was almost invariably held by the Lord Lieutenant (a post dating back to 1569, originally designed to look after the military duties of the county). Although nominally the chief J.P., the Shropshire *custos* in the 17th century rarely took an active part in Quarter Sessions. He was represented there by a deputy *custos*, who probably acted as chairman; the first known deputy *custos*, John Lacon, occurs in 1697. From 1701 comes the first explicit Shropshire mention of a 'chairman'. There was then no formally elected chairman; two or three senior J.P.s were available to take the chair (or sit 'at cushion' to use the local phrase) at any meeting. By 1714, however, Thomas Edwardes was regarded as the usual chairman.

County business

The earliest county rates were those levied at intervals from 1531 onwards to pay for repairs to 'county' bridges. Under an Act of that year any bridge for whose repair no-one could be held responsible became the county's responsibility. In the 16th and 17th centuries the Shropshire county bridges were those at Atcham, Buildwas, and Tern, the Shropshire half of Tenbury bridge, and the western half of Montford bridge; in 1697 the Shropshire half of Chirk bridge was also adopted. Each time a repair was needed, the J.P.s appointed a treasurer to receive the rate money and pay the contractors; the rates were collected for him by the petty constables. The first county rate to be levied regularly was a small one (under an Act of 1572) to give relief to poor prisoners in the county gaol. The first regular county rate of any importance began to be collected under an Act of 1593, in order to provide pensions for Shropshire soldiers injured in the

Crown's service. In Shropshire this 'maimed soldiers' money', as it was called, was administered by two treasurers, both J.P.s; new treasurers were elected annually by Quarter Sessions. Bridges and pensions were thus the J.P.s' earliest important direct public services besides their purely judicial work.

For most of the 17th century the Shropshire county rates were much as they had been in Elizabeth I's reign. Nevertheless the number of men entitled to pensions out of the 'maimed soldiers' money' (the main regular rate) was enormously increased by the Civil Wars. By 1664 the fund was in deficit and its under-treasurer had resorted to taking bribes from applicants in order to make up the losses. In 1668 Quarter Sessions dismissed him and ordered that a new pension should be granted only when an existing pensioner died. There was, too, a natural fall in the numbers eligible to apply: in 1670 there were 205 pensioners, but by 1690 only 140. Thus by the 1690s there was a surplus in the fund, available for other county purposes, and by the early 1700s the pensioners were so few that it had become virtually a general-purpose fund. From 1701 the county was required by statute to levy a recurring rate to pay the expenses of petty constables taking vagrants back to their home parishes.[5] This 'vagrant money' was administered by the same two J.P.-treasurers as the 'soldiers' money', but by 1709 its annual yield was much greater than that of

Much Wenlock Guildhall, where the county Quarter Sessions
met occasionally until the mid 16th century

the soldiers' fund; in that year the soldiers' money was absorbed by the vagrant fund, which thus became the general-purpose county fund. The other principal county rate, the 'bridge money', was levied in 17th-century Shropshire in large irregular sums, which were intended not only to cover immediate repairs but also to maintain a balance so that future urgent repairs would not have to wait for money to be collected. Thus treasurers of the Shropshire bridge money, in theory appointed to handle the proceeds of a single levy, became virtually permanent officers in charge of a standing fund. The bridge treasurer was often a J.P., and could hold office for long periods. Thomas Edwardes, for example, was bridge treasurer from *c*.1697 to at least 1711 and can be regarded as a forerunner of the modern 'county' treasurer.

Petty Sessions
The magistrates' indirect concern for public services had begun in 1536, from which time they were required to supervise the administration of parish poor-rates; this was destined to be an increasingly time-consuming part of their business as parish poor-relief became the subject of more complex legislation. From at least the 16th century the government was anxious to prevent social disturbances arising from poverty; hence the poor-law measures in which the Shropshire J.P.s were involved. The J.P.s also had powers to regulate wages and license traders in food, but in Shropshire they were unable to detect or prevent widespread evasions; most of the time they did not even try. Their efforts to ensure fair prices in the markets were sporadic and short-lived. From 1563 the J.P.s were also required to supervise road repairs, though these were the direct responsibility of the places through which the roads passed. These supervisory duties were usually carried out by 'Petty' Sessions, small groups of J.P.s meeting in agreed divisions of the county. Petty Sessions seem to have originated with the Licensing Act of 1552, which required ale-sellers, to be licensed once a year by any two J.P.s. The ale-sellers naturally applied to the J.P.s living nearest to them, and thus by 1575 licensing divisions (as yet without fixed boundaries, but often following those of hundreds) had begun to form in Shropshire. The J.P.s soon found it convenient to license all the ale-sellers in their division at a single annual sitting, and such sittings were soon found convenient for other routine business such as the supervision of parish highway surveyors and overseers of the poor. Such Petty Sessions were often held either in a magistrate's home or in a local building such as an inn or guildhall.

During the early 17th century, the divisional meetings began to be held at regular monthly intervals. Any difficult or contentious business, however, still had to go to Quarter Sessions.

CHAPTER THREE

The Shropshire Magistracy in the 18th century

Lord Phillips of Sudbury (the former 'Legal Eagle' of Jimmy Young's Radio 2 show) referred to the role of justices of the peace during a debate on the future of the magistracy in the House of Lords on 3 December 2001. He stated that 'from time immemorial, justices of the peace have been the bulwark and personification of local justice'.

Although Lord Phillips was commenting on the present-day position of magistrates, his comments may well have been appreciated by 18th-century justices of the peace. The duties of a magistrate had increased gradually from the mid 16th century, especially in the field of Poor Relief; but during the 'long 18th century' from the 'Glorious Revolution' of 1688 to the fall of Napoléon in 1815, the role of the magistracy of England underwent several fundamental changes, including a gradual but inexorable shift of workload from purely criminal cases to civil duties such as the maintenance of the poor, resettlement of vagrants and responsibility for ensuring that there was no flouting of Sunday trading laws. It has been remarked, with a certain amount of justification, that during the 18th century 'in England everything drifted into the hands of the justices of the peace'.[1] This may be somewhat overstating the situation, but the 18th century undoubtedly saw a transfer of power from the Crown and centralised government to the counties and local bodies. At the same time, other forms of local jurisprudence and social control had lost much of their former powers in the tumultuous preceding century, manorial courts and parish vestries often becoming little more than honorific bodies — a good excuse for an annual formal dinner. In addition, the business of the county was increasingly being conducted behind closed doors; setting the county rates and similar decisions during Quarter Sessions were now not publicly witnessed, whilst there was a concomitant downward delegation of both administrative affairs and summary justice from Quarter Sessions to Petty Sessions (not formally recognised until 1828, but certainly occurring in practice since the 16th century) or to individual justices of the peace. With regard to criminal cases, 'legislation in the 18th century also greatly increased magistrates' jurisdiction for summary convictions'.[2]

Such delegation could occasionally have far-reaching effects; the ill-fated Speenhamland System of poor relief (by which local winter wages of agricultural labourers were supplemented by the parish poor rate, the amount of supplementation being tied to the price of bread and the number of dependants of each labourer) is generally believed to have been instigated in 1795 by a group of magistrates in Speenhamland, Berkshire. The system spread rapidly through much of southern England and Wales (roughly south of a line drawn from Gloucester to Hull), leading to much abuse by employers (many of them magistrates), who were quick to realise that they could cut wages in the knowledge that the parish would theoretically make up the resultant shortfall. Such abuses of a system instigated semi-nationally following a local initiative were heavily criticised from many quarters, including the M.P. for Shrewsbury, Robert Aglionby Slaney, who in February 1831 was questioned on the matter in a House of Lords Committee researching attitudes to the Poor Law. He referred directly to the Speenhamland System:

> I was induced to turn my Attention to what I conceive to be an Abuse of the Practice of the Law in the Southern Districts of England, which appeared to me to have the Effect of lowering the Condition of the Labourers, and lessening the natural Value of their Labour; besides being greatly injurious to them in every Way, it also appeared to me that it was extremely injurious to the Interests of Landed Gentlemen residing in those Districts, for it seemed much dearer to maintain the Poor in the Way they were maintained in some of the Southern Districts of England, than to adopt the better Practice of the North, where Men were well paid. There are Three or Four Abuses which prevail in the Southern Districts of England. In the first place, they pay the Rents of able-bodied Persons out of the Poor's Rate; secondly, an Allowance for the Children (I am always speaking with reference to able-bodied Persons); thirdly, making up the Wages out of the Poor's Rate. This System was adopted in several of the Southern Districts. The Wages were made up to the Number of a Family, according to a fixed and invariable Scale, varying only with the Price of Wheat; in others without a Scale, but still upon the same bad Principle.[3]

It is interesting to note that whilst he commendably expressed concern for 'the condition of the labourer', he was equally quick to point out the detrimental effect that he considered the system to be having on the landed gentry, i.e. his own class. Such criticisms grew inexorably throughout the early decades of the 19th century and led eventually to the New Poor Law being introduced in 1834.

Quality and quantity of magistrates

Richard Burns, a writer and a magistrate, published a guide to the work of a Justice of the Peace in 1755 entitled *Justice of the Peace and Parish Officer*, in which he detailed over 200 various jurisdictions for which they were responsible. The duties of a magistrate therefore could be onerous and complex, if carried out conscientiously. There was often a reluctance on the part of those eligible to take up what could be a considerable burden of office. It has been suggested that only about 40 per cent of those eligible to join the Commission of the Peace actually put their names forward. Of those who did, the necessary degree of conscientiousness was not always present; on 3 July 1793, W. Upton, a magistrates' clerk at Hatton Garden Police Office, memorably wrote to the Home Department stating that, prior to the introduction of stipendiary magistrates, 'had a canine animal brought a shilling in his mouth with a label for specifying his complaint, a Warrant was readily granted'.[4] Admittedly this referred specifically to the situation in London, but there was undoubtedly often a widespread problem in recruiting enough men of the right calibre and dedication to the ranks of the unpaid magistracy.

By contrast, many of those who did serve as magistrates seem to have come to regard it as almost hereditary; G.C. Baugh records that William Cludde of Orleton (died 1765) was a Shropshire magistrate for over 40 years; his son Edward was a magistrate from the 1750s until his death; his son-in-law, Edward Pemberton was a leading magistrate and Chairman of the Bench from 1785–97, and his nephew Thomas Pemberton (see below) and grandson Edward Cludde both continued what had clearly become a family tradition.[5]

A fascinating list survives from 1793 in which the names of all potential candidates for the next Commission of the Peace are given, along with their qualifications or lack of them to serve as magistrates for the county of Shropshire.[6] The list is headed by the Marquis of Stafford, who held a large estate in Shropshire, as did many other aristocrats from outside the county, including the Duke of Bridgwater. Others on the list were not so fortunate; Joshua Blakeway of Lythwood was denied permission to serve as he was found to be a bankrupt, whilst Edward Horne of Leasowes had sold his estate and left the county since the last Commission.

Not only was it difficult on occasion to recruit enough magistrates, it was also extremely hard to punish a Justice of the Peace for misbehaviour. From 1736 only the senior judges of the Kings Bench had 'the power to review magisterial behaviour, and also to punish it criminally', and it was very rare for these powers to be called into use.[7]

Magistrates were appointed by the Crown via the Lord Chancellor, (from the beginning of the 18th century such appointments were made after representations from the Lord Lieutenant of the respective counties) and from the last quarter of the 17th century newly appointed magistrates had to swear oaths of allegiance to the King, the Protestant faith and the office of Justice of the Peace, and then authorise these oaths by taking out a writ of *dedimus potestatem* (literally 'we have given the power'). Such a series of oaths survives from 1738, in which John Bright, Esquire, swore the following in front of Maurice Pugh and Thomas Moore on his appointment as a Justice of the Peace:

> I do hereby promise and swear that I will be faithful and bear true allegiance to his Majesty King George so help me God.

The oaths continued with Bright's hand still placed on the Bible, and after swearing to 'abhor, detest and abjure' Catholicism (memories of the reign of King James II were still fresh in peoples' minds), he was then instructed that:

> Ye shall swear that as Justice of the Peace in the county of Salop in all articled in the King's Commission to you directed ye shall do equal right to the poor and to the rich after your cunning wit and power; and after the Law and customs of this Realm and Statutes thereof made; and ye shall not be at counsel with any person in any quarrel hanging afore you; and that ye hold your Sessions after the form of Statutes thereof made; and that fines [which] shall happen to be made and all forfeitures which shall fall before you, ye shall truly cause to be entered without any concealment or embezzlement and truly send them to the King's Exchequer; ye shall not look for gifts or other cause, but well and truly ye shall do your office as Justice of the Peace in that behalf; and that ye take nothing for your office of Justice of the Peace to be done but of the King's fees accustomed and cost limited by the Statutes; and ye shall not direct or cause to be directed any warrant by you to the parties but ye shall direct them to the Bailiffs of the said county of Salop or other of the King's Officers or Ministers or other indifferent persons to do exactly thereof, so God you help and by the contents of this book.[8]

From 1689 the criteria for becoming a Justice of the Peace were based on a financial qualification of holding land worth a minimum of £20 per year. By 1744 this had increased to a minimum of £100 per year, with the land having to be within the county on whose Commission of Peace the justice wished to be recorded. This qualification clearly ruled out the vast majority of men who held no land and thus had no opportunity to serve their community in this way (women were not admitted to any magistrates' bench in England until 1919, with the first in Shropshire being Mrs. Marion Cock, appointed in 1929). The system thus ensured that it was only men of local importance and financial influence who were appointed as magistrates. Marc du Bombelles, a French diplomat who toured through the English Midlands in 1784, visiting both Bridgnorth and Shrewsbury during his travels, voiced the criticism of many in his diary:

> Several owners of land or merely a house in each county acquire greater authority than the local lord of the manor when they are honoured by being made justices of the peace and this honour is awarded too easily, seeing the importance of their functions, by the lords lieutenant of the counties. The lords lieutenants make this nomination out of politeness for those of their neighbours and acquaintances whom they wish to honour. There are justices of the peace who have this title but do not exercise the functions for which they have sworn an oath.[9]

The position was often regarded by such men as little more than a 'confirmation of their local prestige', and many were content for their names to be included in the Commission of the Peace, without taking the necessary further steps to an executive role within the county.[10] Similarly, of those potential magistrates who did take the necessary oaths, by no means all considered themselves beholden to appear at the Quarter Sessions. In 1701 Richard Gough (1635–1723), author of *Gough's Antiquities of Myddle*, wrote of an anonymous Shropshire magistrate, 'I cannot tell whether he knew where the bench was where the [Quarter] sessions was kept, for I never saw him there'.[11]

Conversely, some magistrates were regarded by their contemporaries as diligent and hard-working, and were clearly held in high regard; Edward Pemberton of Wrockwardine died in December 1800 aged 73, and his entry in the burial register reads:

> An able & upright Magistrate, a man greatly esteemed & beloved, not only in his own Village, but through the whole Neighbourhood. He was accompanied to his grave by many sincere mourners & his loss will be long lamented in a Parish, whose regularity & peace were, in a great measure, preserved by his excellent example & benevolent exertions.[12]

The number of magistrates rose inexorably during the period under discussion, reflecting the increasing judicial duties and also perhaps rising crime figures (although no national criminal statistics are available before 1805, it is generally accepted that the late 17th and the 18th centuries saw a considerable increase in criminal behaviour (and of course the population as a whole was also burgeoning). At the time of William III's accession to the throne in 1688, there were 45 magistrates recorded in Shropshire.[13] By 1721, this rose to 102, 145 in 1733, 249 in 1761, 218 in 1774 (of whom 50 were clergy), 425 in 1793 — this seems to have been a watershed — and by 1830 the situation had stabilised to 297, of whom 95 were members of the clergy.[14]

The increasing percentage of clergymen in the Shropshire magistracy during the period mirrors the general trend in England, but the 1830 figure is high compared to Carl H.E. Zangerl's examination of the returns of justices of the peace for the whole of England and Wales in 1842 (Table 3.1). He found that the magistracy in 1842 was overwhelmingly comprised of the gentry, with the next largest group being the clergy, with the emergent mercantile/middle classes not yet being represented:

Aristocracy	Gentry	Clergy	Middle Classes	Others
8%	77%	13%	0%	1%

Table 3.1 Number of magistrates in England and Wales in 1842 = 3,090[15]

However, he also calculated that in 1831 clerical magistrates made up 28.8 per cent of the total number of magistrates in Wales, and with Shropshire being very much a border county, the situation there may well have been similar. The social and religious composition of the magistracy was not simply a haphazard state of affairs. It has been remarked that 'the politics of the gentry and of magisterial power had a very precise social location', and the Anglican domination amongst the clerical magistrates in Wales and the non-conformist border counties can be seen as a deliberate attempt by the ruling élite to ensure that the views of the Established Church held sway with regard to judicial decisions during a period where the general status of clerics was on the rise.[16]

Duties and work of the magistracy
We have in the previous chapter already heard of some of the business carried out by the Shropshire Magistracy in both Quarter and Petty Sessions. Unfortunately, very few Petty Sessions records survive for Shropshire prior to the mid 19th century, although there is a fascinating *Justice's Book* kept by Thomas Netherton Parker of Sweeney (near Oswestry).[17] This book was handwritten by Parker, who was sworn in as Deputy Lieutenant of Shropshire on 2 November 1803, after previously having held the same post for the county of Worcestershire since 13 November 1796 (he obviously had considerable financial and agrarian interests in both counties). The book details every one of the cases that came before him at his sessions held between 8 March 1805 and 23 July 1813, and contains an interesting cross-section of the work of a fairly active and diligent magistrate. The cases, which run to well over one hundred in number, are all listed with the names of the protagonists and suspects, with a full account being given of Parker's summary judgement on each. The vast majority involve either minor assaults between agricultural labourers or the fleeing from contract by servants and labourers.

For example, on 20 July 1805 Parker adjudged the case of Mary Hughes, a dairymaid who had broken her contract with her employer, Edward Minshall. Mary ran away from her place of employment, and it took the local parish constable Edward Francis three days to locate her and bring her before the magistrate. Parker ordered that Mr. Minshall paid the resultant expenses of 2s. for the drafting of an arrest warrant and the services of the clerk, along with 7s. 6d., being the amount payable to Constable Francis for his three days' search. The total sum of 9s. 6d. was then to be deducted from Mary Hughes' future wages, and she was ordered to continue in Mr. Minshall's service from 31 July 1805 to 11 May 1806. This must have been a severe blow to Mary, the expenses amounting to several weeks' wages.

Such a sum must have seemed large enough to the unhappy dairymaid, but on 18 March 1807, Thomas Netherton Parker imposed a far more severe financial penalty on John Owen of Whittington. Owen fell foul of the notoriously strict Game Laws that had been brought in to protect the 'sporting' interests of the landed gentry and aristocracy. He was obviously a man of some prosperity, as he was found guilty of furnishing one of his servants, John Morgan, with several guns and also of assisting him in laying them in order to take hares from a neighbouring estate. Owen was fined £5 in total, with the sum of 50s. to be surrendered to the Reverend W.W. Davies for the poor of Whittington, costs of 25s. 6d., and 10s. paid in costs to Mr. Lewis Jones (presumably the owner of the land and by extension the hares).

Constable Francis seems to have been diligent and successful in this particular case, but the following year (18 March 1806) he was severely reprimanded by Mr. Parker for failure to carry out several summonses. Parish constables were the mainstay of executive law enforcement in 18th-century Shropshire; as we have seen in the previous chapter there was no organised police force as we would recognise one today until 1836, when Ludlow, Bridgnorth, Oswestry and Shrewsbury formed their respective Borough forces. It was not until 1840 that Shropshire acquired a county force under the leadership of Captain Dawson Mayne, younger brother of Sir Richard Mayne, the first Commissioner of the Metropolitan Police (founded in 1829).[18] Although there has been much recent revision of the efficiency of parish constables, there is no doubt that the general contemporary perception was that they were not the most efficient form of policing. In a Parliamentary Select Committee Report on Policing in 1839, evidence was heard from rural magistrates that:

> As far as our experience extends, we are convinced of the incompetency and inefficiency of the old parish constable. He holds his office generally for a year; he enters upon its duties unwillingly; he knows little what is required of him; is scantily paid for some things, has no remuneration in

many cases; he has local connections, is actuated by personal apprehension, and dreads making himself obnoxious. His private occupation as a farmer or little tradesman engross his time, and, in most cases, render him loath to exertion as a public officer; and all these drawbacks have induced a general persuasion that, in ordinary cases, the parish constable has an interest in keeping out of the way when his services are called for'.[19]

Throughout the whole of the 18th century there was no system of public prosecution; it was the sole responsibility of the victim (or his/her friends or relatives in the case of incapacitation or death) to instigate prosecution of suspects. Although some magistrates did go beyond their duties in investigating crimes, the vast majority played no more part in criminal investigation than hearing the statements of the victim and arranging for the parish constable to search for suspects.[20] Certain costs were refunded to the victim or their representatives

Warrant for the arrest of suspects, 1752
(© Shropshire Archives, 2089/7/5//17)

following a successful prosecution, but as Professor John Beattie has remarked, 'it seems reasonable to assume that poor men must have had to be moved very strongly to bring a prosecution against someone who had assaulted them or stolen from them'.[21]

One of the main duties of the parish constable was to serve warrants on suspects and bring them before a Justice of the Peace for a summary hearing. Such a warrant survives from 1752, issued by magistrate W. Forester:

> To the High and Petty Constables in the Hundred of Bradford South; to each and every one of them, particularly to the constables of Buildwas. This is in His Majesty's name to will and require you, or one of you, upon receipt, hereof, to bring before me or any other of His Majesty's justices of the peace for this County, the body of the desired persons in this list here annexed at the Talbot Inn in Wellington upon Wednesday next, the 22nd inst. to answer to such matters of complaint as will be objected against them by the overseers of the poor of the parish of Buildwas aforesaid and to be examined touching the several places of their last legal settlement. And further to do and receive as to justice appertaineth hereof. Fail not, as you will answer the contrary at your peril. Given under my hand and seal the 17th day of April 1752.[22]

The above cases demonstrate the typical kind of day-to-day judgements given by justices of the peace sitting on their own in fairly informal sessions. Thomas Netherton Parker's *Justice's Book* indicates that he would often go out of his way to try and avoid the cases progressing further up the judicial scale; he was very keen in cases of assaults between individuals for them to settle the disagreement amicably and without further formality, often directing that token damages and a handshake would suffice for the law and the dignity of all parties concerned to be satisfied.

Justices of the peace could also hand out more corporeal forms of punishment; most towns and villages possessed a set of stocks and a whipping post, which were put to use throughout the period. The Guildhall at Much Wenlock still contains both a set of stocks and a whipping post with hand shackles, and an information board records that on 3 January 1766 William Holmes was publicly whipped there for stealing a quantity of leather from the nearby Bedlam Furnace. The stocks remained in use until 1852, with a certain Thomas Lloyd enjoying the dubious privilege of being their last official occupant.[23]

Magistrates occasionally took it upon themselves to promulgate their personal beliefs and political leanings to a wider audience than a Petty Session courtroom. On 31 October 1795 an anonymous 'Country Magistrate' of Shropshire published a handbill entitled 'Five Minutes Advice Before Going To Market', which was aimed at Shropshire's numerous farmers.[24] It was an impassioned appeal to limit

*Whipping post and hand shackles,
Much Wenlock Guildhall*

the price of corn at a time when there was great disquiet about the rapidly rising price (caused by a combination of bad harvests, the French threat and the undoubted profiteering of some producers). The average price of wheat had remained relatively stable during the first half of the century, averaging 34s. 11d. per quarter-hundredweight (28lbs or 12.5 kilos) for the period 1713–1764, but between 1765 and 1800 it rose to 55s. per quarter-hundredweight, reaching a peak of 128s. per quarter-hundredweight in 1800. Some magistrates, aware of the threat to public peace, and no doubt conscious of their own safety, endeavoured to limit the price of staple foods, but often to no avail. Threatening letters were certainly received by magistrates who were also farmers in the neighbouring county of Worcestershire; in September 1812 magistrate and farmer Thomas Biggs of Stourbridge, received the following letter (spelling and punctuation is original):

Mr. Bigges,

Sir,

We right to let you know if you do not a medetley [immediately] see that bread is made cheper you may and all your nebern [neighbouring] farmers expect all your houses rickes barns all fiered and bournd down to the ground. You are a gestes [justice] and see all your felley cretyrs [fellow creatures] starved to death. Pray see for som alterreshon in a mounth or you shall see what shall be the matter.[25]

32

In parts of Shropshire, the populace had previously forced farmers to sell their goods at what was considered to be a reasonable rate; at Halesowen (a detached part of Shropshire until 1844) in September 1766 'they rose, and forced the people to sell cheese at two-pence halfpenny, and flower [*sic*] for 5s. They destroyed two dressing-mills before they dispersed'.[26]

'Five Minute's Advice' was obviously an attempt to forestall a repeat of such occurrences. The writer exhorted the farmers of Shropshire to act wisely:

> As the price of corn is, so will be the price of labour and of every commodity. We have, my friends, a good King, a good constitution, and have had a favourable harvest, all products taken together. Owing to the Troubles on the Continent [the French Revolution was raging], we cannot yet have peace abroad; - but owing to our Sailors, our Soldiers and our Yeomanry, we have quietness at home. Let us then, by a right use of all the means in our power, and especially of our Corn, provide the good and content of each other, which will give us Peace with our neighbours, and above all, acting the dictates of our Conscience, will give us <u>Peace with ourselves</u>.

Whilst the sentiments of the anonymous magistrate were obviously heartfelt, the last decade of the 18th century and the first two decades of the 19th century remained politically and economically turbulent.

However, not all cases that came before the Shropshire magistrates were as serious as those listed above. In January 1772 an unusual case was brought before the magistrates sitting at the Shropshire Quarter Sessions. A True Bill was sworn in court by Edward Acton J.P., stating that a certain John Croxton, a labourer residing in Hope Bowdler:

> In or near the King's Highway, there did erect, put, and place, or cause to be erected, put or placed a certain building called a Bog House, or House of Office, for the reception of dung, human excrement, and other filth.

A Bog House, or House of Office was a primitive toilet (usually an earth closet). The disposal of human waste had been a problem for centuries; since the departure of the Romans in the early 5th century A.D. (who had engineered communal toilets with running water), sanitation had remained at a very basic level. Even castles and royal residences possessed nothing more sophisticated than a 'garderobe' — a small room with a disposal chute usually emptying over a moat. By the middle of the 17th century some private residences had Houses of Offices, but these caused numerous problems; Samuel Pepys recorded in his diary entry for 20th October 1660 that on going into his cellar, 'I put my foot into a great heap of turds, by which I find that Mr. Turner's house of office is full and comes into my cellar, which doth trouble me'.

It is not clear whether the House of Office erected by John Croxton was a private building or a public convenience. There were certainly numerous such public buildings throughout the country by the late 18th century — and there is even a contemporary collection of obscene and humorous graffiti collected from the walls of such buildings.[27] Whichever type of House of Office it was, the indictment records that its erection caused 'divers hurtful, disagreeable and unwholesome smells from the said dung, excrement and filth', leading the air to be 'corrupted and infected to the great damage and common nuisance of all the liege subjects of our said Lord, the King'.

Unfortunately, the verdict of the magistrates is not listed in the surviving records, but it seems unlikely that Mr. Croxton (much in the manner of those unfortunate enough to have been in the vicinity of the illegal House of Office) would have emerged from his court appearance smelling of roses.

Throughout the 18th century, the persistent problem of 'the poor' refused to go away, and in predominantly agricultural counties such as Shropshire, the problem was often exacerbated by the seasonal nature of much of the available work. Magistrates were responsible for much of the immediate administration of the Poor Laws and often issued directions to the various Overseers of the Poor in the parishes in which they held jurisdiction. On 14 April 1741 Thomas Jones, a county magistrate, issued the following judicial decision to the Overseers of the Poor in the parish of Cardington:

> Whereas Louis Edwards, a poor person of your parish came before me this day and made oath that he is not able to subsist himself and family for want of work [… in] your said parish, I do therefore hereby order you, the said officers, to pay unto the said Edwards the sum of two shillings every week until such time as you shall put him to work and that you find his wife hemp or flax to spin according to the instructions in you nomination warranty or until you shall come before me and show cause to the contrary; and hereof fail ye not. Given under my hand and seal this 14th day of April 1741.[28]

The 'instructions in your nomination warranty' refer to the undertakings agreed to by those who were sworn in as Overseers of the Poor by justices of the peace; they swore to provide the able-bodied pauper with work and materials by which the work could be carried out (see above for an example of such a nomination warranty).

They were also responsible for the appointment of the Overseers, as is made apparent in a document dated 11 May 1791, in which magistrate Thomas Pemberton 'appoints Robert Rylands and William Griffiths as Overseers of the Poor, being substantial householders of the parish of Chetwyn[d]' for the period of one year. If the individuals failed to meet on a monthly basis to discuss matters arising from the administration of the poor, then they were 'to forfeit 20 shillings each for each month that you shall be found remiss or careless therein'.[29]

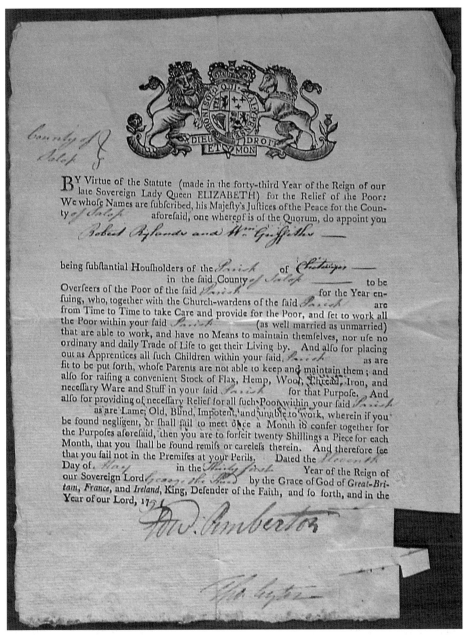

Appointment of Robert Williams and William Griffiths as
Overseers of the Poor for the parish of Chetwynd by Thomas Pemberton J.P.
(© Shropshire Archives, P60/L/1/1)

An agreement sworn between two justices of the peace in 1750 gives a more detailed account of what those who effectively 'farmed' the poor were expected to contribute.[30] The document, dated 1 August 1750, was a tripartite agreement to create a workhouse in the town of Wellington in the parish of Berrington, drawn up between Thomas Hazlehurst, a tailor of Wellington (who was to provide the

Interior of Bridgnorth Town Hall Courthouse
(courtesy of Bridgnorth Town Council)

workhouse), John Kilvert, John Langford, Thomas Kilvert and William Rogers (all Churchwardens and Overseers of the Poor in Berrington parish) and Adam Ottley and Thomas Langley (justices of the peace, who acted as witnesses).

Such provisions were often made between private individuals and representatives of the parish; it was in this way that the first licensed lunatic asylum of the county was created in Bridgnorth in 1792; Joseph Proud was issued a licence to keep 'any number of lunatics not exceeding ten' in his property, and two justices of the peace and a physician were appointed to visit and inspect the premises, with the physician receiving £2 2s., payable out of the £10 cost of the licence.

These ventures must have been considered profitable by those agreeing to undertake them and one hesitates to think of the conditions for many of the recipients of such care. The agreement regarding the establishment of a workhouse stated that

> A public workhouse is provided and set on foot [built] in the said town of Wellington for lodging, keeping and maintaining, setting to work and employing all such poor persons as shall require or desire relief from the said parish of Wellington; and for the better managing and governing thereof, it is thought proper and expedient to set or farm the said Poor ...

This decision followed meetings of the parish vestry (local administrators responsible for the enactment of the Poor Laws) and the consent of the justices of the peace involved in the matter; Thomas Hazlehurst was to provide 'good wholesome and sufficient meat, drink, washing, lodging, wearing apparel and all other Necessaries'. In return he was to be paid the sum of £18 per year, in three instalments in November, February and May.

Such a document shows the important role played by magistrates in the administrative affairs of the county; they oversaw the Poor Law, took a leading part in the judicial process in both criminal and civil law, issued search and arrest warrants, together with a multiplicity of other duties. Occasionally the surviving records suggest a degree of tension between the various magistrates in the county and the various boroughs (incorporated towns with limited independence in administrative and legal matters).

One such document from 1796 details a heartfelt and acrimonious dispute between the bailiffs of the Borough of Bridgnorth and a county magistrate.[31] The dispute arose following the actions of a Mr. Mytton (a county magistrate from just outside Bridgnorth), who sent a summons to the constable of Bridgnorth without consulting the bailiffs. The bailiffs were outraged by this breach of etiquette and convention and fired off a plea for judgement on the issue to Thomas Pemberton, a leading county magistrate (and probably the same Thomas Pemberton who had served as Mayor of Shrewsbury in 1794), in order to obtain a final decision.

The document states that the Borough of Bridgnorth was founded in the reign of Henry VI (1421–1471) and as such was a Royal Peculiar with its own system of justice. The charter from this period stated that the bailiffs and burgesses and their heirs and successors:

> *Shall be Justices of our Peace within the town and liberty and precincts* thereof and shall have for ever full power, correction and authority of inquiry into hearing and determining all matters, complaints, defaults [etc] which to the office of a Justice of the Peace of Labourers and Artificers belong, and other things within the said Town, liberty and precincts thereof arising and happening which in anyway before Justices of our Peace in a county hath or shall have power to enquire and determine. [Neither should] the justices of the peace of Labourers and Artificers of us and our heirs in the said county should in anyway intermeddle … in any thing, cause or article whatsoever to the justices of the peace belonging and pertaining within the said town, suburbs or precincts thereof that from any cause whatsoever arising or happening.

The charter went on to state that a £40 fine would be the result of such interference in Bridgnorth's affairs by any county magistrate — a tremendous sum of money in the 15th century. The bailiffs of Bridgnorth informed Thomas Pemberton that no such 'intermeddling' had before arisen until Mr. Mytton's unwarranted intervention, and asked that 'your opinion is requested whether under the charter of Henry VI the Bailiffs of Bridgnorth retained an exclusive jurisdiction within the town.

Mr. Pemberton replied on 21 April 1796 that 'the county magistrate can have no right to interfere or to exercise any magisterial act within such particular limits. If he does, he subjects himself either to an action of trespass, or in some cases, to an Indictment'.

In 1828 Thomas Pemberton (by then Chairman of the Bench at Shropshire Quarter Sessions) was involved in an entertaining case involving an 18th-century law designed to prevent travelling troupes of actors presenting plays without first obtaining permission from either the Lord Chamberlain or local magistrates.

The *Salopian Journal* of 16th July 1828 reported that at the Shropshire Quarter Sessions a Mr. John Robson had engaged the services of a lawyer, Mr. Wheatley, to ask the court to grant leave for Mr. Robson to perform tragedies, plays and farces at Wellington. Mr. Robson was obviously used to requesting such permission, and presented a petition of '158 respectable inhabitants, who wished that Mr. Robson may be permitted to gratify the public by his performances'. Thomas Pemberton replied that ordinarily, the Bench would have granted permission, but then stated that he had received letters from every magistrate and clergyman in the vicinity of Wellington strongly objecting to the presence of Mr. Robson and his fellow actors. He therefore stated that he would review the case the following day.

It would appear that the Bench (which at that time consisted of 17 magistrates, six of whom were clergymen) took more notice of their colleagues in Wellington than the petitioners. In the Quarter Session Rolls of July 1828, Mr. John Robson appears before the Bench in person charged with staging a play without having obtained their permission. He was brought to court after a complaint from William Keay, a dissenting teacher of Wellington.

The court heard that Robson had staged a performance of Richard Brinsley Sheridan's *Pizarro or The Spaniards in Peru*, in which he had appeared as the Peruvian chief Rolla. Mary Steventon of Wellington affirmed that she had seen the play (which must have been a fairly lavish production, having 18 speaking parts) in a barn at Tan Bank in Wellington. The play apparently lasted over an hour with numerous changes of scenery. Mary Steventon stated that Robson's wife, Harriet had attempted to get round the performance laws by selling two small folded pieces of paper containing tooth-powder for two shillings, and also giving Mary two tickets for the performance. Mrs. Robson was quoted as telling Mary that 'I give you the tickets and sell you the tooth powder', thereby creating the pretence that the performance was not for profit or reward.

Under the Licensing Act of 1737 'every person who shall, for hire, gain or reward, act, represent or perform, or cause to be acted, represented or performed, any interlude, tragedy, comedy, opera, play, or other entertainment of the stage' and who did not have either a legal right of settlement in the place where the performance

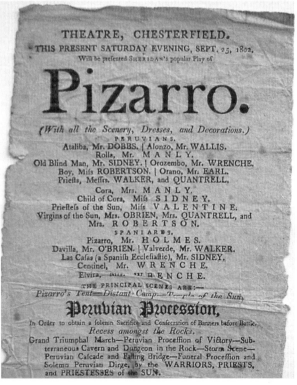

Playbill of 1802 advertising Sheridan's Pizarro or The Spaniards in Peru *(courtesy of Local Studies Department, Chesterfield Library)*

took place or written permission from the king or his representative, the Lord Chamberlain, 'shall be deemed to be a rogue and a vagabond'. Mr. Robson and his fellow actors were therefore taking a considerable risk in staging the play. He pleaded guilty to acting without patent or licence and not receiving the magistrates' permission, but denied doing so for gain, and promptly made a £50 loss with a hefty fine.

Magistrates also often received entreaties from individuals or public bodies to rectify matters such as the non-payment of dues or taxes, as in a letter dated 29 October 1709 from the vicar of St John's Church, Halesowen, the Reverend Thomas Jukes, who complained that several of his parishioners had consistently refused to pay small tithes due to him for a period of two years.[32] He requested that the justices of the peace of Bridgnorth issue warrants of summons to force the non-payers to pay the following fines:

Thomas Millward	2s. 4d.
Humphrey Potter	1s. 4½d.
Joseph Moore	9d.
Humphrey Shipway	9d.
Edward Westwood	6d.

With regard to non-criminal business, two of the most important roles of the 18th-century magistrate were to ensure the removal of vagrants from Shropshire and the maintenance and building of bridges owned by the County. The Vagrants Act of 1700 made the county responsible for any costs incurred in transporting vagrants from Shropshire to their legal place of abode. A list of such costs survives from 7 October 1800, in which the following amounts are detailed:

For conveying Vagrants on foot	1d. per mile
For conveying Vagrants by horse	3d. per mile
For conveying Vagrants by horse or cart	3d. per mile
Lodging	2d. per night
Breakfast	4d.
Dinner	5d.
Supper	7d.[33]

Such costs could obviously add up to a considerable amount depending on the number of vagrants being resettled, and it is therefore perhaps not surprising that vagrancy money was one of the largest drains on the county rates, averaging £296 per year in the 1770s. The first permanent County Treasurer of Shropshire was appointed in 1738 following the introduction of the County Rates Act, when a unified County Rate was also introduced.

Thomas Telford (1757–1834), first County Surveyor of Shropshire
(© Shropshire Archives, PH/S/14/10)

The repair and maintenance of bridges within Shropshire was another considerable burden administered by justices of the peace; over 40 bridges were the responsibility of the county. However, Shropshire was very fortunate (or inspired) in their choice of County Surveyor; they appointed Thomas Telford in the late 1780s. He seems to have enjoyed a reasonable relationship with his employers — although referring to some of the magistrates as 'ignorant and obstinate', he recorded that on the whole they were 'a very respectable bench'.

In 1803 Archdeacon Plymley (himself a Justice of the Peace) in his *General View of the Agriculture of Salop* promulgated his view of the magistracy of Shropshire. He stated that each magistrate should be:

The adviser and peacemaker of his district; he should co-operate in the improvement of rural arts [...] he should set an example of scrupulous obedience to the laws in his own person, and endeavour to sustain the tone of Christian morality throughout his neighbourhood.[34]

It is difficult to assess to what extent the magistrates of 18th-century Shropshire matched up to the Archdeacon's ideal, but what is clear is that their views and actions had considerable influence on the day-to-day functioning of the county. We have seen that the long 18th century saw the rise of local administration centred on justices of the peace. Such a development, 'until it was swept away by the institution of the County Council in the 19th century, conferred on them a power in the counties almost beyond check or challenge'.[35] Such influence and power continued into the 19th century and this is the subject of the next chapter.

CHAPTER FOUR

Policing, Punishment and Social Institutions in the 19th century: the role of the Shropshire Magistracy

In the early part of the 19th century, the Quarter Sessions court involvement in criminal jurisdiction was reduced and the role of the court became more concerned with the administration and finance of the county. As Philips notes, 'for most people, the justices, rather than central government in London, represented public authority as they would experience it in their daily lives'.[1] In the mid 1830s, there were 140 magistrates on the Commission of the Peace in Shropshire, of which about 30 attended Quarter Sessions.[2] From 1842, the numbers of magistrates attending court declined, probably due to the fall in the number of clerical magistrates, and over the next 20 years attendance at court averaged 23, though it grew slightly to an average of 27 by the late 1850s.[3] The numbers of magistrates on the Commission of the Peace between 1863 and 1870 increased to around 150,[4] but only about 40 magistrates were attending Quarter Sessions during the 1862 to 1889 period.[5] Thus a large number of men were listed on the Commission of the Peace but were not active in attending the court.

The Shropshire Quarter Sessions of January 1830 were witness to a trial involving an unusual crime; namely the theft of the hair from 32 cows' tails.

The *Salopian Journal* of 13th January 1830 reported that John Mate, alias John Myatt (the use of an alias indicative that he may have been no stranger to the inside of a court) was indicted on two counts of cutting all the hair off numerous cows' tails. He was first brought before the magistrates to answer a charge of stealing the tail hairs from 18 cows belonging to Mr. Thomas Lloyd of Osbaston in the parish of Kinnersly. Richard Page, cowman to Mr. Lloyd, stated that he had put his master's cows in the cowhouse at 3p.m. on Friday 8th January, but when he came to release them at 6 a.m. the next morning, he found 'the hair of all their tails cut straight off close to the end of the tail'. The second indictment accused John Mate of carrying out a similar attack on 14 cows belonging to Mrs. Hannah Hopkins of Woolston in the parish of Westfelton on the night of Thursday 7th January.

Such mutilation may at first seem simply the actions of a deranged individual, but in fact John Mate was perfectly sane, and had carried out his nefarious activities with a healthy profit in mind. Cows' hair, along with many other types of animal hair, was used in the manufacture of felting for hats. In the evidence heard at his trial, it emerged that he had sold his ill-gotten gains, which amounted to 10lbs. of hair to a local hatter, Mr. Edward Roberts of Oswestry, receiving a total of 5s. 4d. in return — what Mr. Roberts referred to as 'a fair price'.

The hair from the unfortunate cows could not be produced as evidence, having being mixed with other hair at the hatters, but Constable William Franklin of Oswestry testified that he had apprehended Mates at the house of Ann Edwards, 'a person of notoriously bad character'.

As no evidence was produced at the trial, Mates may have escaped the clutches of justice, but he seems to have been overcome by a desire to create an elaborate alibi. The *Salopian Journal* reported that 'there was nothing to bring home the felony to the prisoner until, previous to the case going the Jury, the prisoner was asked in the customary form, whether he wished to say anything for himself'. Mates readily took advantage of the opportunity, and in the words of the newspaper:

> Fortunately for the ends of justice, chose to enter upon a history of his
> travels on the night of the 7th, and of his adventures during the course of
> that night and early the next morning; in doing this he, as many rogues
> have done before, 'let the cat out of the bag', for he gave such an account
> of his buying the hair from a stranger … as left no doubt of his guilt.

Whether or not Mates had spent too much time in the hatters inhaling the mercury fumes that were used in the hatting process (and which drove many hatters insane, leading to the phrase 'as mad as a hatter') is open to question, but Mates was convicted and sentenced to three months' hard labour to be preceded by a public whipping.

The majority of magistrates attending court were landed gentry throughout the period from 1834 to 1889. There were few peers attending court, except for the Earls of Powis and the Herbert and Clive families. The other peers headed the county magistracy, including the second Duke of Sutherland (1839–1845), the second Viscount Hill (1845–1875), and the third Earl of Bradford (1875–1896). The Hills and their friends were highly influential in local government during the mid century and they were strongly supported by the Corbetts of Longnor and their 'weightiest connexions' in county affairs, the Kenyons of Pradoe.[6]

During the 1830s there were seven or eight clerical magistrates attending court, which was about a quarter of those present and reflected their proportion on the commission as a whole. The Conservative Lord Lieutenant Hill strongly disapproved of clerical magistrates, especially those with parochial duties, thus those clergy who attended were close relations of leading landowners.[7] This was with the exception of Reverend Daniel Nihill, he held that there was a 'strict concurrence' between the objectives of the magistrate and the clergyman. He had put this view into practice as governor of Millbank Penitentiary between 1837 and 1843.[8] However, by the mid to late 1860s the numbers of clerical magistrates had increased, although these men were often landowners in their own right, or relatives of leading landowners.[9]

The Chairman of the Shropshire Quarter Sessions court between 1830 and 1850 was Thomas Kenyon. Kenyon and his friend J.A. Lloyd were the 'most influential magistrates' during this period. They dominated the chairmanships of the court's four main committees during the 1830s and 1840s, and Lloyd was nominated as the courts first Deputy Chairman in 1845.[10] J.T. Smitheman Edwardes and Sir Baldwin Leighton were the only magistrates outside the circle of Kenyon and Lloyd's friends and relatives to chair a major committee before 1855. After Lloyd's retirement in 1848, Kenyon, supported by the Hills, nominated Panton Corbett to the position of deputy chairman, much to Sir Baldwin Leighton's displeasure. Again, in 1855 when Panton Corbett resigned the chairmanship, the Hills put forward his nephew Uvedale Corbett in opposition to Leighton, although they were unsuccessful.[11] Leighton wrote in his diary that he 'was exceedingly sorry to find that there had been any division among the Magistrates and [I] certainly would not have accepted the chairmanship had I not thought that the Hills proposed Uvedale Corbett not for his own merits but out of spite to me'.[12]

Leighton was one of the county's most ambitious gentlemen. He took his oath as a magistrate in 1833 and 'applied himself unremittingly to the grind of county business and, eventually to a parliamentary career also'.[13] He regularly attended the Quarter Sessions, holding the position of Chairman from 1855 until he died in 1871, by which time he had only missed three sessions. Prior to this appointment, he had been Chairman of the Quarter Sessions in the neighbouring county of Montgomery from 1844. Leighton opposed the policies and interests of the Hills and their connections; the rivalry between the men in the 1840s and 1850s was described as 'the nearest thing to politics to disturb the court during the period'.[14] After Leighton became chairman, the rivalry with the Hills declined and they were on good terms by 1865.[15]

After Leighton's election as chairman the important committees were chaired by representatives of a less restricted group: Robert Burton,[16] A.C. Heber Percy,[17] John Bather[18] and Moses G. Benson.[19] The Bathers and the Bensons were relative newcomers to landed society, but the Burtons had been seated in Shropshire since the 16th century and Heber Percy's wife inherited the estate at Hodnet in the mid 18th century. The Honourable R.C. Herbert (brother of Lord

Sir Baldwin Leighton
(© Shropshire Archives, PH/S/14/8)

Powis) chaired the Police Committee between 1867 and 1889, and the Kenyon family continued to influence the court throughout the period.[20]

John-Robert Kenyon was deputy chairman during Leighton's long leadership and was elected chairman in 1871 until 1880. When he died, his younger brother Lt.-Col. William Kenyon-Slaney became deputy chairman, then William Layton Lowndes was elected as chairman. However, he was not a landowner and Lord Bradford almost apologised when proposing his election, but reassuring the court that Lord Powis had fully concurred with the recommendation. Lowndes's position as chairman was brief; he resigned suddenly and left the county. Kenyon-Slaney also resigned at this time due to ill-health. The new chairman was Alfred Salwey, who came from a well-established landed family. The deputy elected was Sir Offley Wakeman, an active magistrate in Shropshire for some ten years and who again came from a landed family.[21]

During the 19th century, the social composition of the magistracy in Shropshire remained relatively unchanged, being largely composed of landed gentry, unlike other counties and boroughs that experienced significant changes in the social composition of their benches. Before 1836 the magistracy in the Black Country was dominated by landed society, however by the late 1850s, coal and iron masters, manufacturers, merchants and other men of trade made up over 60 per cent of the bench, while landowners had shrunk to just over one-tenth.[22] In Wolverhampton, 'the forces of urbanisation and industrialisation prompted gradual changes in the composition and ideology of the provincial bench' with the growing dominance of the middle classes on particular benches.[23] Similarly, in Lancashire, cotton manufacturers had begun to be admitted to the bench by the 1840s and 'to a share of local power'.[24]

However, 'not all 19th-century towns experienced a magisterial revolution: in relatively conservative market centres serving rural hinterlands, such as Cheltenham, Lincoln, Exeter and York, changes were slight and continuity was the hallmark of the bench'.[25] Nevertheless, even in Shropshire, by the late 1870s a number of the magistrates were industrialists, professionals, tenant gentry, or lesser landowners, but the numbers were small, about 12 men, although they accounted for just over a third of the average attendance at Quarter Sessions.[26] By the 1880s, this group of men would play a major role in the first County Council.[27]

The Poor Law in Shropshire

Rather than provide a summary of the different unions in the county, this section will focus on the Atcham Poor Law Union, where Sir Baldwin Leighton was an influential and active member of the Board of Guardians. Atcham Union was a union of rural parishes surrounding Shrewsbury (but not including Shrewsbury's six parishes) using the workhouse at Cross Houses near Berrington.[28] Leighton was a particularly influential 'guiding hand', throughout his lifetime and 'took the Atcham union beyond the New Poor Law'.[29] The Union accepted all the rules and suggestions from the Poor Law Commissioners but they also went beyond this, in the interests of both the ratepayers and paupers.

William Day (Assistant Poor Law Commissioner) had brought the Poor Law Amendment Act 1834 to Shropshire in 1836 and recognised that Leighton was the force behind the Union and its policies. He had a 'puzzling admiration' for him, once describing him as a 'man from another century', being forward looking.[30] Soon after 1836, the Union took severe action against its parishes' non-resident paupers living outside the Union. They cut off outdoor relief (relief in the form of money or food and goods and given to paupers living and working in the parish) to paupers in the Atcham Union, or refused to relieve the few Atcham paupers deemed (by Leighton and the Board of Guardians) still worthy of the non-resident relief. The unions in Shropshire's coalfields, and Shrewsbury and Oswestry Incorporations all protested at these measures. By 1838, the workhouse at Crosshouses (where indoor relief was provided) was being used thoroughly as the Union cut down the number of paupers on outdoor relief. The Union's reputation was one of stringency and strictness, outdoor relief policies were central to this image.[31] This may portray an image of severity and a reliance on institutionalisation to cut outdoor relief; however, it is important to point out that whilst Leighton and the Board of Guardians might deny outdoor relief to able-bodied men and women, they would try instead to find them employment.[32]

Other policies, such as denying long-term outdoor relief to orphaned children and deserted wives or children, also demonstrate the way in which the Union sought to mould their policies to the particular group. Walsh notes that in the case of orphaned children, who rarely benefited from outdoor relief which went to their guardians, the Union offered an 'education superior to any afforded by Poor Law authorities in the Kingdom, in a workhouse soon among the cleanest, largest and most professionally staffed in the land.'[33] 'Those who criticised workhouses held their tongues before the Atcham model', the inmates were generously fed, medically cared for, and the children probably received a better upbringing than they would have on outdoor relief.[34] In the cases of deserted wives and children, while they received workhouse relief, the Union and the local magistracy made inquiries after the deserter to move the costs from the ratepayers to those 'responsible'.[35]

Leighton himself had regular contact with the poor, both with his involvement in the courts and magistracy and in the management of his estate. He was personally involved with the poor cottagers and their rent problems, and in a period when landowners were not generally concerned with poor tenants; he was building houses for them, and sought similar action from other owners.[36]

Shelton Lunatic Asylum

The first public institution for pauper lunatics in Shropshire opened in Shelton, Shrewsbury in 1845. The establishment of the institution had been the source of discussion since the late 1830s, when proposed by Leighton and fellow magistrate J.M. Severne. A committee was appointed in 1839, and from 1841 to 1846 the Asylum Visiting Justices' Committee were appointed, both committees chaired by Leighton. He had a great influence on the planning and the building of the asylum and was largely responsible for Montgomeryshire joining the partnership between Shropshire and the borough of Much Wenlock.[37] He also spent considerable time travelling around the country visiting various lunatic asylums, for example, in Lancashire and Dumfries.[38]

Leighton's committee disapproved of the existing provision in the county, which was a combination of out-relief to those who lived in families, those in the workhouses, and two asylums, one at Kingsland, Shrewsbury, and the other at Morda House, Oswestry. Practices at both establishments were criticised; at Kingsland severe cases were kept in damp, dark cells and at Morda, although providing better accommodation, the staffing was inadequate. The Committee also condemned the practice of confining paupers in asylums that were principally run for profit. In their place the committee recommended the establishment of a county asylum.[39]

Dr. Richard Oliver was appointed medical superintendent in 1844; he had some years' interest in the provision of public asylums. However, Leighton had opposed his appointment deeming him 'very ignorant' and inefficient and 'not the sort of person I could act with, with any pleasure to myself'.[40] Leighton twice tried to get Oliver dismissed but eventually it was Leighton who stood down from the committee. He wrote in his diary 'I considered it my best place to decline acting any longer after the next session expired; I certainly felt very much annoyed at thus leaving an establishment which had been erected & opened I may say almost entirely through my own exertions'.[41] He felt that 'where the chairman & the head of the Executive do not work cordially together it is not likely the concern can prosper & under these circumstances I considered the best course for me was to retire'.[42] However, Leighton continued his interest in the field and in the 1860s advocated the establishment of a county lunatic asylum for the middle and upper classes.[43] Despite Leighton's criticisms, Oliver remained the superintendent until 1863.[44]

During the period 1855 to 1877, the Asylum Committee had another 'formidably outspoken chairman',[45] magistrate John Bather.[46] Bather believed that only curable or dangerous patients should be admitted to the asylum, but the poor law guardians in Shropshire were following the lead of the Atcham union and the Lunacy Commissioners who recommended the segregation of imbeciles from the community. In 1863, Bather tried to urge the guardians to confine harmless patients in workhouse wards, due to overcrowding in the asylum and the costs of enlarging the institution. However, the magistrates who were, or had been guardians, namely, Leighton, M.G. Benson[47] and Lt.-Col. T.H. Lovett[48], vigorously opposed his suggestions. Bather too resigned, unable to recommend policies that he found unacceptable.

The establishment of the New Police in Shropshire

Towards the end of the 18th century, there was increased criticism of the old methods of policing, namely, the watchmen and the parish constables, as an effective means of preventing crime in England.[49] The Metropolitan Police Act of 1829 is generally marked as the foundation of a recognisably 'modern' police force. The Acts that followed: the Municipal Corporations Act 1835, and the Rural Constabulary Act 1839, were intended to spread the new police to the provincial boroughs and the counties. However, as Emsley notes, police reform was slow, and despite some forces looking to the Metropolitan model for advice, it was not suitable for all and a variety of models of policing were still being utilised into the 1840s and early 1850s.[50] The County and Borough Police Act 1856 made the establishment of police force obligatory for all local authorities.

The Shropshire Quarter Sessions displayed a 'strong and continuing interest' in the reform of the police in the county from the early 1830s and county policy from 1837 was for the adoption of office constables: 'by 1839 every Shropshire Petty Sessions was a little Bow Street, each with its one (but lone) "runner"'.[51] During the period 1820–1835, Shropshire discussed the need for a constabulary responsible to the Quarter Sessions. In a similar fashion the Cheshire Quarter Sessions had requested an Act to enable them to create a county police force in 1829; such concern showed that 'the local elites were moving on their own', and that policing had become a major concern for the landed gentry.[52]

Shropshire, along with Cheshire, was one of the earliest counties to initiate discussions concerned with police reform. Sir Baldwin Leighton organised a gentry subscription for the hundred of Ford and hired a London policeman William Baxter. In a letter to Edwin Chadwick (Member of the Constabulary Force Commission, 1836–9, one of the architects of the Poor Law [Amendment] Act 1834, and Secretary to the Poor Law Commission), Leighton wrote that the officers' work showed that:

> an extent of depredation of which none of us were before aware, for as tracing offenders occasioned formerly a great loss of time and ... often an expenditure of money, for the parish constable had to be paid, [farmers] seldom took any steps to find out the offender but quietly put up with their loss.[53]

The long records of discussion about county policing demonstrate the main causes of concern to the magistracy. In 1831–2, these focused on striking coal miners from the neighbouring counties of Denbighshire and Flintshire who were trying to bring out Shropshire colliers near Oswestry. The magistrates called on the regular troops, the county Yeomanry, and swore in special constables. The resulting confrontation at Chirk Bridge led to the reading of the Riot Act with three miners being committed to the prison at Shrewsbury.[54] This led the Quarter Sessions to resolve in January 1831:

> that the formation of a Constabulary Force throughout the County ... with a view to the preservation of the Peace and security of property should be adopted, and that this Court strongly recommends the Magistrates ... to take immediate steps with a view to its organisation.[55]

This resolution lapsed, but a year later, the magistrates faced a similar problem of striking colliers on the borders with Staffordshire and Worcestershire. This event led the court again to assert the desirability of a county police force, but once again, the initiative lapsed.[56]

In 1837, Leighton advocated the establishment of a committee to study his experiment of having a paid professional policeman in the hundred of Ford, and argued it had been particularly successful in reducing crime.[57] During the first six months of Baxter's employment it was claimed that only five or six felonies had been committed, whilst in the six months before his appointment 60 felonies had occurred. Baxter had also detected a number of known thieves, who were later convicted and had recovered stolen property of an amount equal to his own salary.[58] Philips and Storch argue that the establishment of small local paid policing initiatives in the early 1830s suggests that the landed gentry were no longer objecting to the principle of a paid force, as long as the force could remain under local and not government control. The Shropshire justices were also in favour of a police force because of the problem of 'roving thieves'. The justices argued that as a Midlands county, Shropshire was particularly vulnerable: it had some industry and mining, bordered similar English and Welsh counties, and contained a number of major roads. They were concerned about 'bands of migratory thieves plundering the unprotected countryside', and Leighton argued that these 'roving thieves' were 'inadequately contained by untrained annually rotating constables'.[59] R.A. Slaney favoured the reform of the police and the Poor Law to protect property and provide general safety. He developed the theme of the county's perceived vulnerable location:

> the position of Shropshire, almost on a direct line from Birmingham to Liverpool and Manchester (in which towns, with London, the most

practiced thieves were reared) exposed the inhabitants to greater injuries from the characters than in more remote districts.[60]

After discussions and correspondence with other counties the Shropshire Quarter Sessions sent a petition to Parliament in January 1838, it stated:

> the Rural Police is at present totally inefficient for the prevention of crime, and ... the detection of it, as the former most important duty is not even attempted, and the latter is ... performed [in Shropshire] by ... office Constables attached to each Petty Sessions .... The passing of an Act to enable the Court of Quarter Sessions to appoint and pay out of the County Rate a body of Constables subject ... to the authority of the Magistrates but placed under the ... superintendence of a Chief Officer responsible to them for the arrangements and disposition of the force ... within the Shire would confer a most important benefit on Rural Districts inasmuch as such as Establishment would effectively provide for the prevention as well as the detection of Offences; for the security of Person and property and for the ... preservation of the Public Peace.[61]

Philips and Storch point out that this particular petition 'contains the precise scheme for the crucial legislation of 1839, which became the framework for English provincial policing (outside the boroughs) into the 20th century'.[62]

In December 1838, the Shropshire Quarter Sessions adopted another resolution, the 'Salop Resolution', which read:

> That in consequence of the present inefficiency of the Constabulary Force, arising from the great increase in population and the extension of trade and commerce of the county, it is the opinion of this Court, that a body of constables appointed by the magistrates, paid out of the County Rate, and disposable at any point of the Shire where their services might be required, would be highly desirable, as providing in the most efficient manner for the prevention as well as the detection of offences, for the security of person and property, and for the constant preservation of the Public Peace.[63]

Russell (then Home Secretary) endorsed this particular resolution, having previously refused to commit to other proposals. This signalled his decision to work with the county government, 'to employ a bona fide provincial initiative to attempt to foster a national consensus among the gentry via the justices of the peace'.[64] This comment also demonstrates that Russell recognised the local power of the magistracy and the need to gain acceptance of the proposals from this group.

Members of Shropshire County Police Force
outside the Shirehall, Shrewsbury c.1860 (© Shropshire Archives)

The Chairman Thomas Kenyon, R.A. Slaney and Sir Baldwin Leighton took the lead in pushing for the establishment of a county police force. In October 1839 the debate led by the aforementioned magistrates and a few other prominent justices led to the unanimous adoption of the County Police Act.[65] Once again, we can identify the prominence of Leighton in the push for the reform of the police force and the influence of other notable magistrates, namely Thomas Kenyon and R.A. Slaney in shaping the crime and policing policies in Shropshire during this period. Shropshire therefore was one of the first counties to adopt the County Police Act 1839; there was no debate on whether to establish a force, rather the discussion was concerned with the cost and size of the force.

In December 1839, a Police Committee was established that was intended to represent the whole of the county and thus had a large membership. From 1857 to 1863, its membership was identical to that of the Finance Committee. In 1863, its Chairman (1861–1864 Colonel William Kenyon-Slaney)[66] stated that it was too large and the committee was reconstituted to include six members elected in court, four ex-officio[67] members and a member from each petty sessional bench.[68]

During the mid 19th century, Leighton was very critical of the administration and command of the Shropshire constabulary. In the late 1850s, he made the position of Chief Constable an uncomfortable one for Captain Dawson Mayne. Leighton was particularly annoyed that Mayne had married a cousin of Sir Rowland Hill, as he strongly disapproved of personal connections between the Chief Constable and the county magistracy.[69]

The County Prison in Shrewsbury

There were six visiting justices to the prison who were appointed at the Quarter Sessions, from the attending magistrates, to act as overseers to the prison. Visiting justices were first appointed by an Act of 1791, but this role was later reasserted in the Gaols Act 1823 and their duties outlined.

The county prison at Shrewsbury was built in 1793. Prison reformer John Howard identified three places of confinement in the town during visits in the 1770s and 1780s: a county gaol, a county bridewell, and a town gaol and bridewell. All of these buildings were inadequate and held only a small number of prisoners. Gaols were primarily places of detention for those offenders awaiting trial, execution, or transportation, and held those imprisoned for debt. Bridewells (or houses of correction) mainly held petty offenders and beggars or vagrants. Often the boundaries blurred between these two places of confinement and they were later amalgamated into 'local prisons' by the Prisons Act 1865. Howard's observations of the prisons in Shrewsbury reflect common problems in prisons during the 18th century. The county gaol, built in 1705, was the largest of the three prisons, holding between 30 and 40 prisoners and debtors when Howard visited. A large proportion of the prisoners were convicts awaiting transportation. Felons and debtors were commonly held together due to the lack of water in the felons' court. Many of the women held were pregnant and although there was a separate court that Howard believed to be for women, it was not in use. There was no infirmary or bath, which Howard thought inadequate, as there had been traces of gaol-fever in previous years, and it would not protect against small-pox and other diseases. However, there was an apothecary available, who could order the gaoler to provide a better diet for a sick prisoner.[70]

The county bridewell was on the same site as the county gaol, but legally it was a separate building, and only held a handful of prisoners. There was only one day-room for men and women, and a workroom. Above these rooms were two rooms for women, where Howard observed one woman who was 'languishing on the floor in a consumption'.[71] The night-room for men was in a dungeon down ten steps and there was a small court for water. Prisoners were able to attend a public worship in the chapel on Sunday, which Howard considered a privilege not available in many bridewells. However, there was little or no employment and half of any profit made from employment went to the bridewell keeper.

At the town gaol and bridewell, Howard found a plaque inscribed 'In this house the poor of the town are set to work — He that will not labour let him not

The Front Court of the County Gaol, Shrewsbury, 1791.
This satirical print lampoons the lack of security and poor conditions at
the old County Gaol, built in 1705. A = A prisoner breaks through the roof
and makes his getaway onto an adjoining building. B = A prisoner is tied
to a post for stealing bread from another inmate. C = Amy Butcher, a local
greengrocer, cries her wares within the courtyard. D = A highwayman slips a
contraband letter into his wife's pockets. E = A pickpocket is plying his trade.
(©Shropshire Archives, 503/6)

eat. An. Dom. 1636'.[72] The building consisted of sundry rooms on two floors over a gateway. There was a small court, although no sewer or water (this was supplied in nearby houses), and no employment.

In 1785, the county gaol was presented as insufficient and plans were made for a new prison amalgamating all three of the pre-existing institutions into one site.[73] The new prison was the work of commissioners appointed under a local Act; these were leading magistrates with an interest in prison administration: William Smith, Rev. Edmund Dana and Rowland Hunt. The construction of the new prison seems to have been rooted in the nationwide interest in 'prison reform' at the end of the 18th century. John Howard certainly had a profound influence on the local magistrates, who had a bust of the reformer placed over the new gatehouse to the prison. But then Howard was a close friend of Rowland Hunt and frequently visited both Shrewsbury and Boreatton Park, Hunt's estate.[74]

The prominent prison architect William Blackburn, and local surveyor John Hiriam Haycock designed the new prison with the disciplinary system of

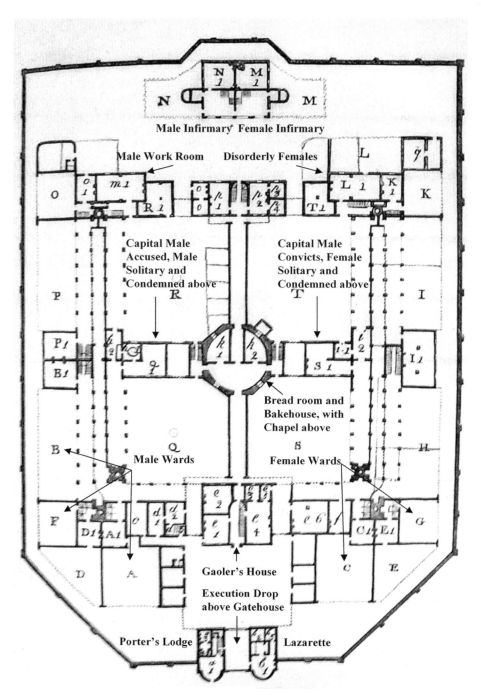

Male Infirmary Female Infirmary

Male Work Room   Disorderly Females

Capital Male
Accused, Male
Solitary and
Condemned above

Capital Male
Convicts, Female
Solitary and
Condemned above

Bread room and
Bakehouse, with
Chapel above

Male Wards   Female Wards

Gaoler's House

Execution Drop
above Gatehouse

Porter's Lodge   Lazarette

Ground-floor plan of Shrewbury County Prison, 1797
(© Shropshire Archives)

The imposing façade of the County Prison, Shrewsbury, constructed by Thomas Telford, with a bust of John Howard above the entrance door

'classified association' in mind — whereby the prisoners were divided according to their gender and their offence, and were held in different rooms or areas of the prison known as courts. This can be seen more clearly on the plan of the prison from 1797. The construction of the prison then fell to the first county surveyor, Thomas Telford.[75]

The Gaols Act 1823 enacted this disciplinary regime, forbade the use of alcohol and advocated the benefits of religious and educational instruction, appointing chaplains and improving facilities for instruction.

By the 1830s, the prominent debate in prison management across the country, and in America, was between two disciplinary regimes, the separate system and the silent system. Under the separate system, prisoners would spend all of their time in their cells: working, sleeping or eating. Prisoners attended chapel and exercise, but this was the only time that there were allowed out of the cells. Even then they would have their faces covered, or exercise in specially constructed airing yards to avoid recognizing, or conversing with other prisoners. Under the silent system, prisoners would work in association but they were to maintain silence at all times. Each of these systems were advocated by various leading magistrates and contemporary commentators as the most appropriate method for reforming prisoners and allowing them to reflect on their criminal activities. Both systems also hoped to reduce the possibility of 'contamination'; young or first offenders should be prevented from conversing with hardened offenders and becoming worse members of society because of their imprisonment.

The Prisons Act of 1835 established government inspectors of prisons. The first two inspectors were Rev. Whitworth Russell and William Crawford both of whom were strong advocates of the separate system and wrote extensively about its merits in their third report to the Home Secretary. The Prisons Act of 1839 regularised the use of the separate system in all prisons throughout the country.

The visiting justices at Shrewsbury prison had already started to experiment with the separate system in 1837, believing it was the best means of achieving discipline and control. The magistrates were initially reluctant to proceed without directions from the government, but having not received any communications from the Home Office they decided to begin the experiment.[76] In 1837, they began experimenting on a small scale with the separate system, initially building five separate cells. They were unable to adopt the system for the whole of the prison due to the expense of providing a large and well-ventilated cell for each prisoner. However, gradually the justices began to convert the corridors and various wings of the prison to the separate system.

By 1842, there had been further expansion of the separate system, 35 cells had been in use for three-and-a-half years, the average period of imprisonment in them had been three months; the longest stay of any one prisoner ten months. All of the officers unanimously supported the system. The chaplain said separate confinement was more favourable to education, religious and moral improvement, and in no way injuriously affected the prisoners' minds.[77] The surgeon thought the health of the prisoners in the separate cells was better than for those prisoners held in the common courts. The governor argued that the prisoners under the separate system were more orderly, less tempted to break prison rules, and 'less obnoxious to punishment'.[78] He remarked that 'the comparatively innocent were not liable to be annoyed or corrupted, by communication with more hardened offenders, and that the latter had ample and uninterrupted opportunities for reflecting on their past lives, and a chance therefore, for reformation'.[79]

This process of slowly converting wings or sections of the prison continued over the next two decades. In October 1864, a further 72 cells were built and on their completion the whole of the prison had been converted to the separate system. In total, there were then 194 separate cells, 171 for male prisoners, 23 for females and an additional three punishment cells.[80] However, by this time, the separate system had lost its reformatory aims and deterrence or retributive punishment had become the dominant penal philosophy of the period. The separate cells were retained in the deterrent regime but were part of a policy of 'hard labour, hard board, hard fare', where harsh living conditions, strict dietary regulations and hard labour combined to achieve the necessary deterrent discipline aspired to by the Caernarvon Committee in 1863 and embodied in the Prisons Act of 1865. Edmund Du Cane, Chairman of the Prison Commission, later refined this approach and developed a national penology that he applied to all local prisons that came under his control in 1877, when they were nationalised.[81]

Those Shropshire magistrates who were most active in the administration of the prison between 1840 and 1877 were predominantly landed gentry and many came from families that were long established in county society. Those magistrates most frequently appointed were Sir Baldwin Leighton (as Chairman of the Quarter Session), Reverend Henry Burton, Charles Montgomery Campbell, Colonel William Kenyon (who became Kenyon-Slaney), William Butler Lloyd, A.C. Heber Percy, Thomas H. Sandford, Charles Spencer Lloyd and William Layton Lowndes.[82] To these we can add those magistrates most active in the period 1871 to 1878, the Chairman of the Quarter Session, John-Robert Kenyon QC, together with the Reverend Edward Warter, Thomas Slaney Eyton and John Loxdale.

A number of these gentlemen were Deputy Lieutenants of the county, a position described by the Webbs as 'one of purely social dignity', or held office as High Sheriff.[83] Four of the 13 gentlemen were chairman or deputy chairman of the quarter sessions and therefore would have been ex-officio members of the other quarter sessions' committees. Thus, through their participation in other committees,[84] or their family relations to other prominent committee members, these men were particularly influential in the establishment and administration of the criminal justice system and local government in 19th-century Shropshire.[85]

Juvenile Reformatory

King and Noel point out that from 'the mid 17th to the late 18th century contemporary commentators rarely regarded young offenders as a separate, distinct problem'.[86] Different methods of responding to young offenders only began in the 19th century. During the next century, 'juvenile delinquency was established as a major social problem, and a focus of great anxiety amongst the propertied'.[87] There was 'a major transition in the attitudes to, and the policies towards young offenders'.[88] New legislation changed the way in which juveniles were tried for offences from the mid century. Nationally penal developments in the 1830s and 1840s shifted the attention from the nature of the offence to an emphasis on individual reformation. The new generation of prison governors and chaplains found the 'ever-increasing numbers of children ... an embarrassing impediment to reform', and they questioned the policies used and indeed, whether prisons were suitable places for children at all.[89] The magistrates in Shropshire were also concerned about the treatment of juvenile offenders in prison.

In 1847, the county prison's visiting justices' book shows a copy of a petition in favour of the proposed Juvenile Offenders Bill, at the time before Parliament. The magistrates showed their satisfaction with the objectives in the preamble of the Bill, namely 'to ensure the more speedy trial of juvenile offenders and to avoid the evils of their long term imprisonment previously to Trial'.[90] Indeed, 'for many years there had been attempts to separate youthful offenders from other prisoners, to provide special regimes for them and, if possible, to keep them out of prison altogether'.[91] Many commentators voiced similar concerns, for example, the Brougham Committee of 1847 argued that 'the contamination of a gaol … as usually managed may often prove fatal, and must always be hurtful to boys committed for a first offence, and thus for a very trifling act they may become trained in the worst of crimes'.[92]

In the early 1850s, the visiting justices at Shrewsbury received a communication from the Philanthropic Farm School relating to the reformation of juvenile offenders.[93] The average number of juvenile offenders under the age of 16 committed to Shrewsbury prison in the preceding five years, was 75 per year. However, during the year beginning Michaelmas 1850, the number had increased; 46 had been committed up to this time (April 1851). Set against this the term of imprisonment for juveniles was generally short and there were not a large number of juveniles in the prison at any one time. The justices agreed that where possible juveniles should be separated from older offenders, but this was difficult to carry out unless they were confined alone. The justices, however, feared that separate confinement was not suited to the minds of youth, and were concerned that serious injury to the offenders' intellect may result from lengthy periods of confinement. They feared less hardened boys could be more contaminated if placed in a ward with other juveniles, rather than with selected adults, as currently occurred. They therefore recommended that in cases where it was necessary to commit a juvenile offender on a summary conviction to prison, this should be for a short term and that males under 14 should be whipped to deter them from future offences.[94]

The Philanthropic Society also suggested giving magistrates the power to make relatives of juvenile offenders' pay for their support in prison. The justices thought this beneficial, and that 'no doubt in London and other large towns cases do occur frequently where the parents are in good circumstances and have neglected their offspring'.[95] However they noted that in Shropshire that when a relative could be discovered, they were often among the poorest classes in the county, and that the system would therefore be inoperable locally.

The Philanthropic Society also suggested lengthening the terms of imprisonment for second and third offences. However, if the sentences were to be passed in county gaols then the justices could not agree with the proposal. They thought boys required different management from adults and unless they were transferred to a prison like Parkhurst, or an institution like the Philanthropic Farm, the juveniles would stand very little chance of reformation.[96] The magistrates believed that if theses sentences were passed in gaols then they would probably leave in a worse state of mind than when they entered.[97]

The visiting justices agreed with the society that power should be vested to send juvenile offenders, who were orphaned or deserted, to some Reformatory. They also agreed that the Directors of these establishments should have certain powers of detention. However, they felt that the County or the Borough should not be liable for the expense of maintaining juveniles and suggested that the Union or Parish should be charged with a portion of the cost.[98]

In 1854 a Committee was appointed to consider the possibility of forming a Reformatory Institution for juvenile offenders in Shropshire.[99] They duly deemed it desirable to have somewhere to send juvenile offenders, but that it was not advisable to erect an institution for Shropshire alone. They considered whether the county should unite with some of those adjoining in establishing such an institution. Hitherto, about £58 per year was available for sending prisoners to the reformatory and this sum had been sufficient. Nevertheless, the justices hoped that the Gaol Charity would receive an increase in subscriptions, as magistrates and the public had become more aware of the problem.

The Committee also recommended the formation of District Pauper Schools, distinct from prisons or Union Workhouses. They argued that by having a large number of children together, education, religious and moral training could be given in a more efficient manner, and at less financial cost. They believed that 'by removing the Pauper child from the contamination, which under the present system in too many instances surround him, a great check may be given to crime'.[100]

During the next quarter, eight juvenile offenders were committed to the prison and one female prisoner was sent to a Philanthropic Society.[101] The magistrates also gave their support to a petition regarding District Schools that was subsequently presented to the House of Commons:[102]

> The petitioners, both from judicial and general acquaintance with the subject of juvenile delinquency are led to the conviction that, with a view to due protection of the public from depredation and to rescue children from ruin by precluding their growth in criminal habits, which in their future career may be formidable to society, legislation measures, more comprehensive and effectual than at present exist, are becoming highly expedient.[103]

They submitted results from experiments that supported the compulsory formation of such schools. The petition ended by requesting the House of Commons to pass a Bill both for the prevention of crime and the reformation of juvenile offenders by means of pauper district schools and Reformatories.[104]

At an adjourned session further discussions resolved that the County should unite with another county, or private individuals to establish a Reformatory[105] and a Committee was appointed to communicate with interested parties.[106] This Committee visited the Reformatory at Saltley, which was established to receive juvenile offenders from Birmingham and Warwickshire and subsequently inquired whether they would allow Shropshire to unite with them, as the buildings were about to be enlarged. The committee also requested the Court to give them an estimate of the sums likely to be raised by voluntary subscriptions and that a public meeting or circulars should be sent to those most likely to assist.[107] At the June Session 1856, it was reported that 21 boys had been sent to Reformatories in the preceding 16 years according to a Return provided by the gaol chaplain. Of the 21 boys, four had been apprenticed, three had emigrated, and two had runaway. Two of the boys were sent home 'unfit for Refuge', four had been transported, one was 'living by stealing', and one had died. The remaining four boys were still in the reformatory.

The amount of money subscribed towards providing a Reformatory in the county had by then reached £827 11s., not enough to erect an establishment for the County alone. The Committee recommended that a circular be sent to the subscribers requesting them to pay up their subscriptions, the sum to then be invested in either Government Funds or on the security of the County Rates. The interest on this amount should then be paid to the Gaol Charity Fund and used to send boys from the prison to Reformatories. They also recommended that in cases where the committing magistrate sent a juvenile to a reformatory, instead of prison, he should be remanded in the gaol, and the chaplain should arrange to send the boy to a Reformatory.[108]

There were also problems caused by magistrates sending juveniles to the prison to be whipped. Juveniles could be sent to the prison for this punishment without any sentence of imprisonment, and in such cases, delays sometimes occurred in obtaining the Surgeon immediately, thus a short sentence of imprisonment should be given as well.[109]

In the summer of 1858 the visiting justices finally entered into an agreement with the Philanthropic Society. They agreed to pay 2s. 6d. per week for maintenance and 1s. for rent for each male juvenile offender under the age of 14. They were limited to sending only six boys in the subsequent 12 months and to no more than 12 boys at one time.[110]

In 1857 the visiting justices' reports began to record the number of juvenile offenders who were committed each quarter. The average number of juveniles per year, committed under the Juvenile Offenders Act 1847,[111] is shown in Table 4.1.[112] The table shows a fluctuation in the numbers between 1858 and 1863, between a low of 9.3 and high of 11.6. Then there is a sharp rise in the average number of juveniles committed under the Act that peaked at 19.6 in 1871. The average number then declines to 10 in 1876, rising slightly to 13 in 1877.

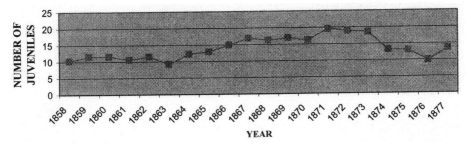

Table 4.1: Number of Juveniles committed under Juvenile Offenders Act 1847 from 1858 to 1877

As McConville has indicated in the *Oxford History of the Prison*, reformatory and industrial schools did reduce, but not stop the flow of juvenile offenders to prison. The reformatory school sentence was not a direct substitute for prison, and legislation stipulated that the reformatory sentence be preceded by a prison sentence of less than 14 days. Then the reformatories kept the boys out of prison by removing them from circulation. McConville maintains that young offenders frequently spent long periods in prison before reformatory places were found for them.[113] This may also have been the case at Shrewsbury as the justices were constrained by the limited numbers of boys they could send to the reformatory. McConville concludes that by the end of the 1870s, reformatories and non-custodial sentences had developed further, and the proportion of prisoners under the age of 16 was largely reduced.[114]

Conclusion

During the 19th century, the county magistracy had a vital role in the administration of local government. The magistrates discussed in this chapter were particularly proactive in the establishment and administration of various social, policing and punishment policies in the county. Along with Cheshire, Shropshire was one of the first counties to initiate discussion concerned with establishing a county police force, and with regard to the poor law and the county lunatic asylum, the magistrates moved with national policy and sought to established policies they saw a fit for the needs of the county. With regard to imprisonment, magistrates in Shropshire were active in initiating the building of a new prison early in the 'reform' period and built the prison to hold prisoners under classified association, later enforced by the Gaols Act 1823. The visiting justices who administered the prison in the 1830s began to operate a small number of separate cells even before the system had been regularised by the Prison Act of 1839. Although, it was not until the 1860s that the whole prison had been converted to the system, this nevertheless illustrates their proactive involvement in the establishment of prison disciplinary regimes.

CHAPTER FIVE

The 20th century and beyond: the future of the Bench

'never use the Bench as a place from which to show off
your wit or your learning'
Earl Jowitt (Lord Chancellor 1945–51)[1]

It may seem strange to say that the historian of the 20th-century Bench does not enjoy the advantages that historians of earlier periods possess, but that is the case. As the courts came to deal with more and more types of crime, and many more offenders towards the end of the 19th century, the whole system was enlarged to encompass increased numbers of individuals sitting as magistrates. By the middle of the 20th century there started an accelerating movement towards a more professional magistracy which gathered pace as the century continued. Both of these processes, which are discussed later in this chapter, considerably increased the amount of administration and bureaucracy in the court system. Many thousands of documents were created which recorded committee decisions, policies and practices. However, these have never been public documents, and it is true to say that the processes of local justice have become more opaque and privatised as time has gone on. The magistracy itself has striven to publicise its activities through visits to schools and workplaces (through 'Magistrates in the Community' projects), and has also democratised to the extent that it is no longer populated solely by the great and the good (though they are not of course excluded).[2] Nevertheless, the processes of local justice have perhaps become more distant to the general public in the early 21st century than ever before. Certainly the public galleries in today's courthouses are not bulging with audiences that hoots, applauds or laughs their way through cases as they did in the 19th and 20th centuries. Moreover, today's magistrates are private individuals, whilst the magistrates described in the previous chapters — Thomas Horde, Thomas Netherton Parker or Sir Baldwin Leighton for example — can be traced in the newspapers or records of public bodies because of their substantial involvement in the affairs of the county, indeed the country.

Historians of the recent past therefore struggle to find adequate sources that can reveal the workings of the 20th-century courts. It is for that reason that we are grateful to the magistrates and retired ex-magistrates who volunteered to be interviewed for this chapter so as to 'put some flesh on the bones' of the official records that we have surveyed.[3] This chapter aims to cover the history of the bench over approximately 100 years by exploring contemporary issues faced by the magistracy today. In other words, it examines how we have arrived at the present situation, and what may lie in the future.

The changing patterns of crime

The pace of development in Shropshire was not as dramatic as it was in some areas of England, and it maintains a very rural identity to this day. The populations of the major towns grew in the late 19th century and early 20th century, as did the regional capital, Shrewsbury. The town was a commercial and retail centre which served a rural hinterland, and, at least until recent years, developed at a steady and comfortable pace. In many respects, the Shropshire towns and villages remain the same rural communities, virtually unchanged from the late 18th century. This is also true of the courts. As previous chapters have described, court houses and building used for judicial business have existed for centuries in Shropshire; for example Bishop's Castle Town Hall built in 1745–50, Bridgnorth Town Hall built

Ludlow Guildhall

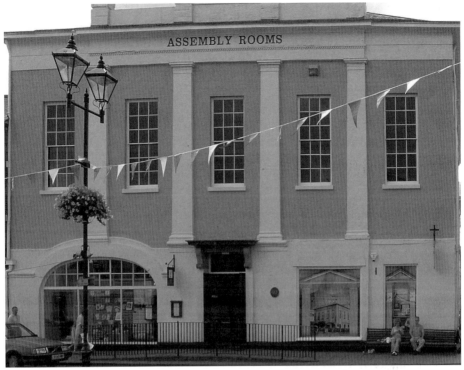

Ludlow Assembly Rooms

in 1648–52 and Ludlow Guildhall, a 15th-century building extended in 1774–6. However, as the population grew in the county, the 19th century witnessed the establishment of many more courthouses, some purpose built, some adapted from existing residences or county buildings. The courts listed below (and these are just a selection of courts built in the county in this period) are dated from the time that courts regularly sat:[4] Ellesmere Town Hall (1833), Ludlow Assembly Rooms (1840), Newport Town Hall (originally built 1615, but moved to new Town Hall in 1860), Shifnal Magistrates Office (1840), Shrewsbury Market Hall

Shrewsbury Market Hall

(1871), Shrewsbury Shire Hall (1833, replacing earlier Shire Halls, enlarged in 1908), Shrewsbury Judges' Lodgings (1821), Wellington Police buildings (1853, enlarged 1892), Wenlock Guildhall (renovated and enlarged in 19th century).

The availability of local courts, and the introduction of official police services into Shropshire, both tended to increase the number of cases brought before the magistrates towards the end of the 19th century (see Fig. 5.1).

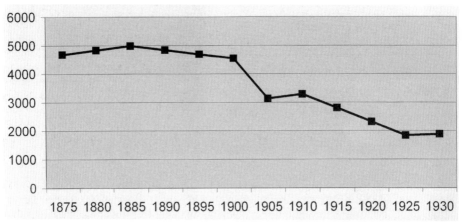

Fig. 5.1 Number of cases brought before Shropshire magistrates, 1875–1930

However, by the turn of the century, there was a marked downturn, with the number of prosecutions practically halving between 1875 and 1930. The decline in prosecuted violence is notable (see Fig. 5.2), and there was also a large decline in drunkenness, although the numbers were still quite high (see Fig. 5.3).

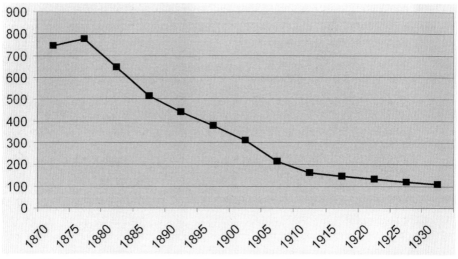

Fig. 5.2 Prosecutions for violent offences, Shropshire, 1875–1930

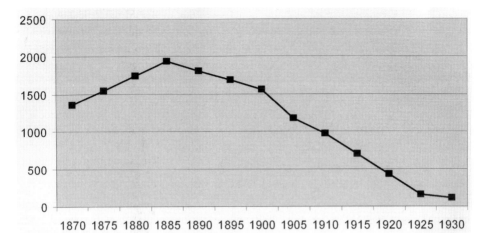

Fig. 5.3 Prosecutions for drunkenness and disorderliness, Shropshire, 1875–1930

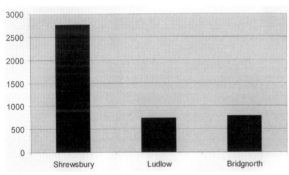

Fig. 5.4 All prosecutions, Shrewsbury, Ludlow and Bridgnorth, 1870–1885

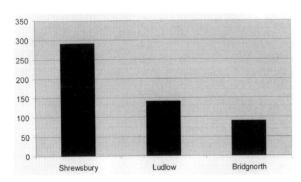

Fig. 5.5 Violence against the person, Shrewsbury, Ludlow and Bridgnorth, 1870–1885

Within Shropshire itself there were significant differences, and Shrewsbury, being the most populated area, exhibits the largest prosecution rates (in all categories of crime). As can be seen in Figs. 5.4, 5.5 and 5.6, the Ludlow and Bridgnorth figures added together do not make up the amount of crime in Shrewsbury, and, in the case of drunkenness, they do not get anywhere near Shrewsbury's level.

Despite Shrewsbury's relatively high level of drunkenness compared to its Shropshire neighbours, crime in Shropshire appeared to be relatively low in the 1930s and 1940s. Where had all the crime gone to, and were magistrates just

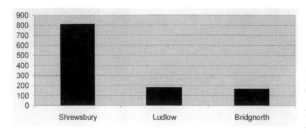

Fig. 5.6 Drunkenness, Shrewsbury, Ludlow and Bridgnorth, 1870–1885

left twiddling their thumbs? The category of crime missing from our figures is that of regulatory offences — including Public Health Acts, as a former magistrate recalls:

> Certainly at Bishops Castle and Church Stretton, a lot of it was failing to dip sheep. I mean we had a lot of that sort of thing. Failing to clean out cattle lorries. These sorts of things don't come into the courts any more because they don't fail to dip sheep anymore. I remember the first case that I sat on was someone building a barn; more than a barn, a sort of hangar, without planning permission … a lot of agriculture things. And petty, petty cases. A bit of theft here and there … but no, there were a couple of murders, and I sat on committal [serious 'indictable only' cases such as these are always sent to the Crown Court]. But in the beginning it was the sort of low crime you expect from a small town.

The largest number of prosecutions, however, involved motoring offences. The enormous growth in motorists and in motoring offences kept the magistrates in Shropshire, and elsewhere very busy indeed. 'In 1900, six years after the first vehicle appeared on the road, transgressions of the law constituted just four cases in a thousand found guilty in magistrates' courts. By 1930, with a little over two million vehicles on the road, they accounted for 43% of all non-indictable offences and had passed 60% by the time war broke out'.[5] Today, approximately 13,000 motoring offences are prosecuted every day.[6] Most towns in Shropshire had major roads running through them, and magistrates from Oswestry, Ludlow and Church Stretton in particular were plagued with speeding motorists.

Life in the courts
There was tremendous variation in Shropshire courts in the mid-20th century, from the grand and imposing to the cosy and compact, but the procedures were the same in each. A bench of magistrates (usually three but sometimes more) would preside from a raised stage, in front of them a clerk who took notes and issued legal advice when asked to do so. In the dock, the defendants faced questions from police prosecutors, normally a sergeant specially trained for this role, and hoped for the best.

Shropshire, being a rural county experienced problems with 'incomers'. The hop-pickers who arrived to carry out seasonal harvest work were a thirsty bunch, and no doubt many of the pub fights that ended up in court began with arguments between locals and seasonal workers. The other group that found themselves in the dock were the gentleman of the road; a magistrate recalls that:

> Tramps were committing petty offences. They would walk down a road and take a bottle of milk off the doorstep and drink it, it was that sort of thing. And I remember one who was a particular problem, so we arranged he would go to a hostel and we spent about two hours on the phone finding him a place in Shrewsbury, which he promised to go to, definitely promised to go to … and I was driving along next morning and I saw him on the Hereford Road!

Another elderly tramp looked to the courts when the weather turned nasty:

> He lived in a broken down shed near the river in Ludlow. When it got cold he needed a bit of warmth. So he would ring up the police station and say 'I've been knocked down in Broad Street and I'm lying in the road, so come and get me'. He didn't mind if it was a hospital or a cell as long as he had somewhere to go. They would bring him in occasionally for wasting police time. But it was pointless really …

Many of the regulatory offences (public health acts, animal regulation offences, and so on) were no longer making it to the courts by the 1970s, not being seen as police matters. The main offences (after 1985) prosecuted by the Crown Prosecution Service were petty thefts (mainly motivated by drug use), drunkenness, criminal damage and minor violence (both these last offences are often alcohol-related), as recalled by former magistrates:

> We always got the same families. The same large families … people who wouldn't pay for a television licence … we had the odd brawl or whatever. Perhaps the odd affray. But we never had any serious problems [in Oswestry].

> There were always a sort of element of trouble makers in Ludlow [in the 1970s and 1980s] and it would always spill out after they had been in various clubs … and there would be different families who would be at one another's throats and they would go and have a drink, then there would be fisticuffs … then somebody looks at someone the wrong way, and off it goes again.

The Shropshire bench is and always has been a comparatively small one, especially given the geographical area it covers. In 2005 there are approximately

Oswestry Magistrates Court

226 J.P.s in the county (Telford and Bridgnorth 106; Ludlow 14; Shrewsbury 60; Oswestry 24 and Market Drayton 22). Perhaps for that reason, the overwhelming feel of the Shropshire bench — from the small courts, the sense of belonging engendered amongst court users, the familiarity with 'problem families', juvenile offenders, and local tramps, and the objective of assisting as well as punishing offenders – is one of local knowledge and affiliation:

> I always felt that parents would take more charge of their children if they knew they should come up before a juvenile court facing people they knew. They would find it embarrassing. They would make sure their children behaved themselves, so they weren't put in that embarrassing situation.

> There was a sense of belonging with the probation service, we had a quarterly meeting with them, and it was very meaningful. Now, it's just another training session. When I was first appointed [in the 1960s] you used the probation officer to befriend and help and support, and often you wish you could do that now. It wasn't a punishment as such, and we used probation officers to help people to sort themselves out … but that close contact with the probation service has been lost.

The ability of the Shropshire courts to maintain a sense of local justice, and having a duty of care over victims of crime, offenders, and the local community, is one of the strongest assets of a local system of justice. However, new national and even international trends may impact on the Shropshire courts in the future.

Contemporary issues for Shropshire magistrates

Lay and professional magistrates
Unpaid volunteers who have received no formal legal training deal with the vast majority of criminal prosecutions (some 98%), legal advice being provided by advisors with legal qualifications. This 'lay' bench now constitutes nearly 30,000 magistrates. There is also a very small group of paid legally trained magistrates sitting mainly in metropolitan areas. Stipendiary justices (now called District Judges) had been first appointed in London in the 18th century, and later spread to the major cities as the volume of prosecutions increased.[7] In Shropshire stipendiaries from neighbouring counties had been brought in on a few occasions in the 1980s, but it was only in 1994 that a stipendiary based in Telford was appointed. Now the region known as West Mercia has one District Judge (appointed in 2001) who is based in Worcester. However, in Shropshire, as elsewhere, there has been constant discussion around the efficiency of paid and unpaid justices.

Lay justices are still slower than their professional colleagues, according to a recent study.[8] However, in the last few years, government-set targets on dealing with offenders, and administrative changes have tended to increase the efficiency of the courts in any case. For example, 'Narey' courts introduced in the 1990s divided prosecutions into those defendants who promptly pleaded guilty and could be sentenced without delay, and those defendants who pleaded not guilty or required time to take legal advice.[9] This not only allowed cases to be processed more quickly, but also meant that defendants were placed before the courts very quickly (within three days usually). Before this reform was introduced trials could take place over a year after the alleged offence had taken place. There are also now strict targets for dealing quickly with both juvenile offenders, and also 'career' criminals (prolific offenders).

It is also said that lay benches are also less consistent in their sentencing than stipendiaries. This has, perhaps, some unintended consequences. Lay benches are more likely to use their local knowledge to impose a sentence which may not be the one recommended in the guidelines issued by the Judicial Studies Board (possibly imposing tougher penalties when there is a particular problem that they wish to address e.g. drunkenness in town centres; or more lenient sentences where they know the problems and life situation of a particular offender). Local magistrates may be less receptive to new sentencing policies or practices that are produced in line with government wishes. They could, in these respects, be considered to act undemocratically at times, however it would be difficult to imagine that local people would want it any other way. Although it would simply be inaccurate to accuse stipendiaries of machine-justice, it is true that lay benches do not impose custody anywhere as near as frequently as stipendiaries, or when the guidelines recommend it. Indeed, research on three benches in the North Midlands showed that lay magistrates viewed custody simply as a punishment and was therefore of limited use in rehabilitating offenders, reserving it for the most serious cases.[10]

So, there are differences between the lay and professional bodies, but many magistrates today feel that the gap is narrowing, and that they are indeed becoming a semi-professional bench. One reason for this view is the increase in training. Magistrates appointed in the 1950s and '60s received very scant training before sitting. Aubrey De Vere Beauclerk, for example, was added to the Commission of the Peace on 7th September 1965, and just over a month later sat on his first panel at Oswestry. In the 1960s magistrates undertook ten hours of training over a five month period, rather than the many hours of training provided today, and whereas Earl Jowitt could only suggest that magistrates visit remand homes and local prisons in 1961, twenty years later visits became mandatory and were arranged as a matter of course for new magistrates.[11]

New magistrates in Shropshire and West Mercia now have three full days of training and observe two or three courts in operation before they first sit in court. Established magistrates undergo training on a regular basis, and the additional duties of mentoring new magistrates, and appraising existing magistrates adds considerably to the training and monitoring duties carried out. Some fear that the necessary burden of training magistrates is not only changing the character of the lay bench, but also damaging the ability of the service to attract new members, particularly those in full-time work, and the self-employed. If that happens, how will it alter the representative nature of the bench?

Representation

'The office of Justice of the Peace is not a reward for past services to the community. It involves an important job of work, which has to be done and done efficiently' remarked Lord Kilmuir in 1951. In the same advice book issued to new magistrates in 1961, Earl Jowitt reiterated that 'nothing is more important for the stability of our institutions, nor can there be any stronger bulwark of our liberty, than the fair and impartial administration of justice'.[12] That principle is thought best guaranteed by a bench which is representative of the local community. As has been stated in previous chapters, the ranks of the magistracy had always been stocked with the landed families and their offspring. Magistrates were required to have land with a rentable value of £100 a year, which made it an exclusive club.[13] That qualification was removed in the early 20th century, and there has been a gradual increase in diversity on the bench. In Shropshire, the landed estates are still well represented. The Acton family, for example, has been heavily involved in local affairs for centuries. Tom Acton's father, who was a J.P., was asked whether his son was ready to join the bench and Tom subsequently received a letter from the Lord Chancellor telling him that he had been appointed (in the 1960s). Tom's grandfather had been appointed a magistrate in 1883, and during the First World War had also served as the Acting Chief Constable whilst the Chief Constable was at the Front. Tom himself served as a magistrate for many years (eventually becoming Chairman of the Ludlow bench).

Shropshire may be one of the few counties where the landed estates are represented to such an extent, but the courts still maintain diversity with people from all walks of life, and there have been various milestones on the route to a representative bench, including the appointment of Shropshire's first female magistrate in 1929. Female magistrates were, it seems treated as exotic specimens in the early days, and were expected to conform to current modes of femininity. Hats were to be worn by women in court at all times until the 1970s, and it wasn't until near the end of the 20th century that female magistrates wore trousers without complaint or comment. The acceptance of female magistrates, no matter how competent, was a slow affair, as a female magistrate appointed in the 1970s recalls:

> And my very first morning of sitting, I walked in and one of the magistrates, a male magistrate said, 'Well, I think you are too young and I certainly wouldn't like to be judged by a young person like you, particularly a woman'. … We sat as five magistrates and the closer to the Chairman the more influence you had. And if the Chairman didn't think that a young female had anything to offer, they didn't talk to you, they didn't actually talk to you.'

The late-20th century has witnessed a refocusing by legal scholars and criminologists on the issue of judicial bias in the magistrates' courts. Various writers have raised concerns that the sentencing of women, the poor, the young, and ethnic minorities in Britain is unjustly harsh; and, that in part, this state of affairs has arisen because the social and political composition of the magistrates' benches do not match the economic, race and other demographic profiles of the communities they judge.[14] The system is still not perfect, and ethnic minorities in particular are under-represented in magistrates' courts generally. In Shropshire the situation is better. The 1991 census showed a 1.6% ethnic minority population figure for the county (including Telford and Wrekin), with 2.3% of the magistracy from ethnic minority backgrounds. No doubt the balancing of the bench by gender, political orientation, occupation and other demographic factors has been made possible by a more regulated system of appointment.

Applicants to the bench can nominate themselves or be nominated, and, if selected, face two interviews with an advisory body. This is a vastly different scenario from even 20 years ago, as a former magistrate recalls:

> We didn't have interviews in the way that magistrates do now. I had a telephone call to say that the Chairman of Ludlow bench would come and interview me at home. And we sat and we had coffee, and we talked about gardening, and I'm a very keen embroiderer so we talked a lot about that. And we had a very pleasant morning. And as she was going, I said 'Well, is there anything I should know about being a magistrate, if I am a magistrate?' And she said 'Don't commit a motoring offence, dear'.

The benches in Shropshire are now balanced politically, with female magistrates slightly outnumbering males. All magistrates appointed to the Shropshire benches are drawn from, and have strong connections with, the local communities they serve, but the interview process is far more rigorous than ever it was.

Local v. National justice
In the mid-20th century there were 35 separate magistrates courts in Shropshire, that were divided in the early 1950s into six divisions — Ludlow, New Drayton, New Wrekin, New Mid-Shropshire, Oswestry, and Bridgnorth. The guiding principles for the reorganisation were that the principal market towns would be preferred because of their accessibility, because they were recognised as civic centres, and because of the available accommodation they could provide busy courts. Nevertheless, a programme of improvement was needed to ensure that magistrates no longer had to sit in draughty courts in their overcoats, as recorded by a Clerk in 1953, who stated that: 'I always advised any magistrate appointed to Church Stretton to wrap up warmly in the winter'.[15]

The first meeting of the 26 members of the Shropshire Magistrates Courts Committee (MCC) met on 29th February 1952. Nearly 50 years later, in 2001, the Shropshire, Hereford and Worcester Courts Committees merged to form the West Mercia Magistrates Courts Committee, with the same responsibilities but over a much-enlarged geographical area. Whilst solely Shropshire justices had managed the courts there had been considerable updating of courts in the county. In the 1970s a new court suite was added to the Bridgnorth Council premises. Ludlow court remained at the Guildhall but underwent a substantial programme of refurbishment, as did Market Drayton. A number of courts were amalgamated

The Silvester Horne Institute, Church Stretton — where Petty Sessions were held in the 1920s

Shrewsbury Magistrates Court

in 1984 into the Telford courts, and placed adjacent to the police station, and Oswestry court was moved into sumptuous surroundings. Shrewsbury court had a large purpose-built premises completed in 1994. However, there was also a programme of closing courts where they were felt to be too small to be viable, or where the size of the local population did not warrant a court. These closures and amalgamations of benches were deeply unpopular amongst local magistrates. In 2005 there are five magistrates' courthouses still in use: Telford (now including Bridgnorth magistrates), Ludlow, Shrewsbury, Oswestry and Market Drayton.[16]

The MCC itself faced organisational changes itself in 2005. As part of a national programme to amalgamate the administration of Magistrates, Crown and County courts into one unitary authority, the West Mercia MCC, together with every other MCC, was abolished in April 2005. The replacement body, Her Majesty's Court Service, is currently responsible for ensuring the courts are efficiently organised. Although organised in 42 areas within five regions, there is a growing trend towards establishing national criminal justice agencies. Magistrates are not now appointed to the county and can sit anywhere in England or Wales; the prison and probation services have recently been reconfigured into the National Offender Management Service; the training of magistrates is becoming organised on an area and regional rather than county basis, and may become a national organisation in the near future. Similarly the agenda set for the courts is more and more becoming dominated by concerns of national government, to the concern of some magistrates:

> there's too much outside interference from the Home Office, the Lord Chancellor's Department, imposing conditions … whoever was imposing conditions hadn't got the faintest idea of what things were like in Shropshire.

The recent changes in the administration of the local Shropshire courts and the tendency to centralise court services might help to shape the magistracy of the future. In 2003 the Lord Lieutenant, Algernon Heber-Percy J.P., instigated a consultation about the future of the courts in Shropshire and after the consultation it was agreed that there should only be two benches in Shropshire: Telford and South Shropshire (Telford, Bridgnorth and Ludlow) and Shrewsbury and North Shropshire (Shrewsbury, Oswestry and Market Drayton). The smaller courthouses of Ludlow, Oswestry and Market Drayton were to remain in use and therefore the distribution of justice to remain more or less 'local'. These amalgamations were due to be operational from January 2006, but the introduction of the 2003 Courts Act has meant that the consultation period has to be repeated, with discussions continuing between Her Majesty's Court Service West Mercia Area Management team and the Department of Constitutional Affairs.

The last five chairmen of the Shrewsbury bench.
From left to right: Catherine Trimby, chairman 2003–06;
Anthony Hollings, chairman 1994–99; Frank Leah, chairman 1986–91;
Judy Townsend, chairman 1999–2003; John Wall, chairman 1991–94

The Future of the Bench?

In 1948 a Royal Commission entertained the possibility of replacing the lay bench with a professional body. One committee member, Lord Merthyr, remarked that, 'I think it is merely a question of time before lay justices disappear. It is a question not of whether but when they should be replaced.'[17] However, the idea was dropped when the committee decided that 500 lawyers of sufficiently high quality could not be found to replace the lay benches.[18] They did, nevertheless, recommend some changes, notably the establishment of joint sittings of stipendiaries and lay magistrates, an idea resurrected by Lord Justice Auld in his report on the 21st-century bench (again, the idea came to nothing).[19]

Some 50 years after the Royal Commission, Rod Morgan, a noted criminologist and Chair of the Youth Justice Board, noted that the start of the 21st century was a time of 'great uncertainty about the future of the magistrates' courts'.[20] He should know, as he had been commissioned by the government to carry out a review of the efficiency and legitimacy of the lay magistracy.[21] However, his recommendations, which many lay magistrates had awaited with some trepidation, did not suggest that the lay principle be put to one side, rather he gave an equivocal view of the merits of lay and professional benches. His report together with the studies of justice and sentencing carried out by Auld and Halliday in the same year all contributed to a vibrant discussion about the future direction of the magistracy.[22]

The various studies and reviews all made it clear that the replacement of the lay bench would encompass massive financial, political, and social costs, and for those reasons alone (let alone questions of local choice and issues of legitimacy) it is unlikely to happen in the near future. Indeed, it would not be surprising if the replacement of a lay bench was still being discussed a century from now. It is also very unlikely that the British system will harmonise with continental Europe to produce inquisitorial courts (with magistrates conducting enquiries rather than hearing cases presented). Nevertheless, there are still likely to be other substantial changes. For example, the drive to professionalisation and specialisation is likely to continue, with increasing levels of training in legal procedures, new sentences, and methods of dealing with offenders. It is also possible that, with people living longer, the maximum age limit of 70 could be extended; and, at the other end, the government are keen to draw in younger people as magistrates (and have reduced the minimum age to 18). Moreover, considering the difficulties in recruiting people of working age, in full time employment, it is not beyond the bounds of possibility that the qualification of magistrates having no convictions could also fall by the wayside. A third of all men have a conviction by the time they are 30 years old and that does not include motoring offences. At present, anyone who has a conviction of any kind is virtually barred from joining the magistracy. Although a distant and controversial prospect, it is just possible that this prohibition could be relaxed.

So it seems that the Shropshire magistracy has had a venerable history, and has served the people of Shropshire for centuries with distinction and diligence. No doubt, in one form or another, magistrates living in Shropshire will continue to serve the local community for the foreseeable future.

Further Reading

Barrett, A., and C. Harrison, *Crime and Punishment in England* (London: UCL Press, 1999)

Baugh, G.C., (ed.), Victoria *County History of Shropshire Vol. III* (Oxford: Oxford University Press for the Institute of Historical Research, 1979)

Beattie, J.M., *Crime and the Courts in England 1660–1800* (Oxford: OUP, 1986)

Eastwood, David, *Government and Community in the English Provinces 1700–1870* (Basingstoke: Macmillan, 1997)

Carlen, P., *Magistrates' Justice* (London: Martin Robertson, 1976)

Darbyshire, P., 'Magistrates', in McConville, M. and G. Wilson, *The Handbook of the Criminal Justice Process* (Oxford: Oxford University Press, 2002)

Dignam, J., and A. Wynne, '"A microcosm of the local community?": Reflections on the composition of the magistracy in a petty sessional division in the North Midlands', in *British Journal of Criminology*, Vol. 3, no.2, 1997

Hawkings, David T., *Criminal Ancestors: A Guide to Historical Criminal Records in England and Wales* (Stroud: Sutton Publishing, 1996)

Landau, Norma, (ed.), *Law, Crime and English Society* 1660–1830 (Cambridge: CUP, 2002)

Parker, H., M. Sumner, and G. Jarvis, *Unmasking the Magistrates* (Milton Keynes: Open University Press, 1989)

Philips, David, *Crime and Authority in Victorian England: the Black Country, 1835–60* (London: Croom Helm, 1977)

Rawlings, Philip, *Policing: A short history* (Cullompton: Willan Press, 2002)

Seago, P., C. Walker and D. Wall, 'The development of the professional magistracy in England and Wales', in *Criminal Law Review*, 2000, 631-651

Skyrme, Sir T., *History of the Justices of the Peace* (Chichester: Barry Rose, 1994)

References

Chapter 1 The English Magistracy Past and Present
1. E. Moir, *The Justice of the Peace* (London, 1969), pp. 15-16. For the emergence of the Justice of the Peace during the medieval period, see also A. Musson, *Public Order and Law Enforcement: The Local Administration of Criminal Justice, 1294-1350* (Woodbridge, 1995); A. Musson & W. M. Ormrod, *The Evolution of English Justice: Law, Politics and Society in the Fourteenth Century* (London, 1999); J. Bellamy, *Crime and Public Order in the Later Middle Ages* (London, 1973).
2. A. Harding, *The Law Courts of Medieval England* (London, 1973), pp. 93-5.
3. Moir, *The Justice of the Peace*, pp. 20-1.
4. J. Briggs, C. Harrison, A. McInnes & D. Vincent (eds.), *Crime and Punishment in England: An Introductory History* (London, 1996), p. 48.
5. Moir, *The Justice of the Peace*, pp. 29-30. For the study of crime and law enforcement in early modern England, see especially J. S. Cockburn (ed.), *Crime in England, 1550-1800* (London, 1977); J. A. Sharpe, *Crime in Early Modern England, 1550-1700* (London, 1984); J. Brewer & J. Styles (eds.), *An Ungovernable People: The English and their Law in the Seventeenth and Eighteenth Centuries* (London, 1980); Alan Macfarlane, *The Justice and the Mare's Ale: Law and Disorder in Seventeenth-Century England* (Oxford, 1981).
6. S & B. Webb, *English Local Government: The Parish and the County* (1906; London, 1963), pp. 295-7.
7. Moir, *The Justice of the Peace*, pp. 42-3; 50.
8. Webbs, *The Parish and the County*, pp. 298-99.
9. *Ibid.,* pp. 300-1.
10. Moir, *The Justice of the Peace*, pp. 167-74.
11. K. Wrightson, 'Two concepts of order: justices, constables and jurymen in seventeenth-century England', in Brewer & Styles, *An Ungovernable People*, pp. 21-46.
12. F. W. Maitland, *Justice and Peace* (London, 1885), p.80.
13. See, for example, D. Hay, 'Property, Authority and the Criminal Law' in D. Hay, P. Linebaugh, J. Rule, E. P. Thompson & C. Winslow, *Albion's Fatal Tree: Crime and Society in Eighteenth-Century England* (London, 1975), pp. 17-64.
14. Webbs, *The Parish and the County*, p. 320.
15. For further details, see especially N. Landau, *The Justices of the Peace, 1679-1760* (Berkeley and Los Angeles, 1984).
16. *Ibid.,* p. 342.
17. F. McLynn, *Crime and Punishment in Eighteenth-Century England* (Oxford, 1989), pp. 31-5. See also P. Rawlings, *Policing: A Short History* (Cullompton, 2002), Ch. 4, 'The professionalization of policing, 1660-1800', pp. 61-105.
18. *Ibid.,* p. 344-7.
19. See, for example, the description of Mr Justice Gobble in Tobias Smollett, *Sir Lancelot Greaves* (London, 1762), p. 90.
20. See, for example, the characterisation of Parson Adams in Henry Fielding, *The Adventures of Joseph Andrews* (London, 1742) and of Squire Weston in Henry Fielding, *The History of Tom Jones* (London, 1750).
21. Moir, *The Justice of the Peace*, pp. 82-4.
22. Webbs, *The Parish and the County*, pp. 350-3; Moir, pp. 106-7.
23. B. Keith Lucas, *The Unreformed Local Government System* (London, 1980), p. 49.
24. *Ibid.,* p. 68.
25. *Ibid.,* p. 54.
26. Moir, pp. 102-130.

27. See, for example, J. Saunders, 'Magistrates and Madmen: Segregating the Criminally Insane in Late-Nineteenth Century Warwickshire', in V. Bailey (ed.), *Policing and Punishment in Nineteenth Century Britain* (London, 1981), pp. 217-41; S. McConville, 'Frustrated Executives: A Lost Opportunity of the English Magistracy', *Victorian Studies*, 33, 4 (1990), pp. 581-602.

28. For further details, see Dorothy Marshall, 'The Role of the Justice of the Peace in Social Administration', in H. Hearder & H. Lyon (eds.), *British Government and Administration* (Cardiff, 1974), pp. 155-68. See also Keith Lucas, *The Unreformed Local Government System*, pp. 57-60.

29. Marshall, 'The Role of the Justice of the Peace', p.168.

30. For the study of the relationship between popular protest and public order during this period, the classic texts include E. P. Thompson, *The Making of the English Working Class* (London, 1963); F. O. Darvall, *Popular Disturbances and Public Order in Regency England* (Oxford, 1934); E. J. Hobsbawm & G. Rude, *Captain Swing* (London, 1969); F. C. Mather, *Public Order in the Age of the Chartists* (Manchester, 1959); J. Stevenson & R. Quinault (eds.), *Popular Protest and Public Order* (London, 1974); J. Stevenson, *Popular Disturbances in England, 1700-1870* (London, 1979); S. H. Palmer, *Police and Protest in England and Ireland, 1780-1850* (Cambridge, 1988).

31. See, for example, D. Taylor, *Crime, Policing and Punishment in England, 1750-1914* (London, 1998), pp. 7-26.

32. For further details, see Moir, pp. 131-149.

33. See, for example, R. Swift, 'Urban Policing in Early Victorian England, 1835-56: A Reappraisal', *History*, 73, 238 (June 1988), pp. 211-237; C. Emsley, *The English Police: A Political and Social History* (London, 1991), pp. 24-42.

34. D. Philips, 'A 'Weak' State? The English State, the Magistracy and the Reform of Policing in the 1830s', *English Historical Review*, CXIX, 483 (Sept., 2004), pp. 873-891; See also D. Philips & R. D. Storch, *Policing Provincial England, 1829-1856: The Politics of Reform* (London, 1999), pp.136-166.

35. D. Foster, *The Rural Constabulary Act 1839: National Legislation and the Problems of Enforcement* (London, 1982), pp.18-41; Philips & Storch, *Policing Provincial England*, pp. 85-92.

36. D. Fraser (ed.), *Municipal Reform and the Industrial City* (Leicester, 1982), pp. 1-12.

37. Moir, pp. 179-80.

38. *Ibid.,* p. 182.

39. Staffordshire County Record Office, Lieutenancy Papers, Outletter Book of Lord Talbot 1822-42, 19 September 1835: Talbot informed Lord John Russell, the Home Secretary, that 'the rule has been in this county not to place gentlemen in the Commission of the Peace who are in trade as they might be called upon to adjudicate in cases in which they have an interest'.

40. D. Philips, 'The Black Country Magistracy, 1835-60', *Midland History*, 3 (1976), pp. 161- 90.

41. C. Zangerl, ' The Social Composition of the County Magistracy in England and Wales, 1831-81', *Journal of British Studies*, 2, 1 (1971), pp. 113-25.

42. R. Swift, 'The English Urban Magistracy and the Administration of Justice during the Early Nineteenth Century: Wolverhampton, 1815-60', *Midland History*, 17 (1992), pp.75-92. See also D. Woods, 'The Operation of the Master and Servant Act in the Black Country, 1858-75', *Midland History*, 7 (1982), pp. 93-115.

43. B. Godfrey, 'Judicial Impartiality and the use of Criminal Law against Labour', *Crime, History and Societies*, 3, 2 (1999), pp. 57-72; B. Godfrey, 'Law, Factory Discipline and 'Theft': The Impact of the Factory on Workplace Appropriation in Mid to Late Nineteenth Century Yorkshire', *British Journal of Criminology*, 3,1 (1999) [Special Issue: *Histories of Crime and Modernity*], pp. 56-71.

44. For further details, see Moir, pp. 182-197.

45. A number of internet sites provide useful information about the current nature, activities and responsibilities of the magistracy. See for example:
http://www.magistrates-association.org.uk
http:// www.obv.org.uk/magistrate
http://www.bbc.c.uk/crime/fighters/magistratescourt.shtml

Chapter 2 Shropshire Justice of the Peace before the 18th century

1. Barrett, A. anmd C. Harrison, *Crime and Puishment in England* (London, UCL Press, 1999), pp. 9-15.
2. See below, Chapter Four for further details on the history of policing in Shropshire.
3. Lemon, Sir Robert (ed.), *Calendar of State Papers, Domestic Series Elizabeth 1581–90* (London: Longman, 1865), letter dated 1st March 1583, Vol. CLIX. Sir Francis Walsingham was one of the most feared men in Elizabethan England, being Secretary of State and the head of Elizabeth's counter-espionage service.
4. Letter reproduced on the Internet at www.oldarcadia.com/sidney_letters.html.
5. See below, Chapter Three for an example of such rates.

Chapter 3 The Shropshire Magistracy in the 18th century

1. Hammond, J. L., and Barbara Hammond, *The Village Labourer 1760-1832: A Study in the Government of England before the Reform Bill*, 4th edition, 2 vols. (London: Guild Books, 1948), vol. i, p. 13.
2. David Phillips, 'Dread of the Crown Office; the English Magistracy and Kings Bench 1740-1800', *Law, Crime and English Society 1660-1800*, ed. Norma Landau (Cambridge: C.U.P., 2002), p. 20.
3. *Journal of the House of Lords: volume 63: 1830-1831*, 'Appendix: Poor Laws: 18 February 1831'.
4. National Archives Home Office Records HO 42/26, f.28.
5. G.C. Baugh, 'County Government 1714-1834', *Victoria County History of Shropshire vol iii*, ed. G. C. Baugh (Oxford: Oxford University Press for the Institute of Historical Research, 1979) [from now referred to as *VCH: Shropshire*, 1979, III], pp. 115-14, p. 117. The Victoria County History series remains the most comprehensively researched authority on the history of Shropshire.
6. Shropshire Archives QS/8/4/1 *Observations to the list for the New Commission of the Peace 1793*.
7. David Phillips, 'Dread of the Crown Office; the English Magistracy and Kings Bench 1740-1800', *Law, Crime and English Society 1660-1800*, ed. Norma Landau (Cambridge: C.U.P., 2002), p. 19.
8. Shropshire Archives 3053/4/3 *Oath Subscribed by John Bright Esq. Before Maurice Pugh and Thomas Moore, on appointment as Justice of the Peace 1738*.
9. Hunt, Joseph, ed., *Bombelles in Britain: the diary kept by a French Diplomat during a visit to Midland England from August 4th to September 10th 1784* (Birmingham: J. Hunt, undated), pp. 33-34.
10. Beattie, J. M., *Crime and the Courts in England 1660-1800* (Oxford: OUP, 1986), p. 59. This book remains a seminal work on the early modern courts of England, containing a wealth of information regarding all aspects of magisterial duties and behaviour.
11. Quoted in D. C. Cox, 'County Government 1603-1714', *VCH: Shropshire*, 1979, III, pp. 90-114, p. 95.
12. Entry in Wrockwardine Parish Register quoted in Shropshire Archives 665/5969, notes on letter sent by FS to Mrs. Pennington, Ashburnham Place, near Battle, Sussex, 20 March 1801.

13. D.C. Cox, 'County Government 1603-1714', *VCH: Shropshire*, 1979, III, pp. 90-134, p. 92.

14. G.C. Baugh, 'County Government 1714-1834', *VCH: Shropshire*, 1979, III, pp. 115-14, p. 116.

15. Carl H.E. Zangerl, 'The Social Composition of the County Magistracy in England and Wales, 1831-1887', *Journal of British Studies* XI (November 1971), pp. 113-25.

16. Eastwood, David, *Government and Community in the English Provinces 1700-1870* (Basingstoke: Macmillan, 1997), p. 96.

17. Shropshire Archives 1060/168-170 Justice's Book 1805-1813.

18. For a historical compendium of all police forces of Britain, see Stallion, Martin, and David S. Wall, *The British Police: Police Forces and Chief Officers 1829-2000* (Bramshill: Police History Society, 1999).

19. *Crime and Punishment Police vol. VIII (IUP Reprints Series): First Report on the Constabulary Force in England and Wales PP 1839 (169) vol. XIX.*

20. For a fascinating account of the detective efforts of one magistrate, see John Styles, 'An Eighteenth Century Magistrate as Detective: Samuel Lister of Little Horton', *Bradford Antiquary* New Series Part XLVII (October 1982), pp. 98-117.

21. Beattie, J.M., *Crime and the Courts in England 1660-1800* (Oxford: OUP, 1986), p. 47.

22. Shropshire Archives 2089/7/5/17 Order of J.P., 17 April 1752.

23. Anon, *The Guildhall, Much Wenlock* (Much Wenlock Town Council Information Leaflet).

24. Shropshire Archives 665/4/1361 A Country Magistrate, 'Five Minutes Advice Before Going To Market', 1795.

25. *Hue & Cry*, 6 February 1813. *Hue & Cry* (later renamed the *Police Gazette*) was a newspaper containing details of crimes that had occurred throughout England and which were reported by provincial victims or magistrates. It was founded in 1773 by Sir John Fielding, Chief Magistrate at Bow Street Police Office, and was sent out to every County Magistrate and County Gaol. Shropshire Archives are, to the best of my knowledge, unique in possessing the first editions of the newspaper from 1773-1780 (the time of Fielding's death). Nearly every copy has a report missing, neatly cut-out, presumably removed by a Shropshire magistrate who closely followed any cases reported from Shropshire. For a fuller account of food riots in the Black Country, see David J. Cox, 'Civil Unrest in the Black Country 1766-1816', *Family and Local History Yearbook, 9th edition* (Nether Poppleton: Robert Blatchford Publishing Ltd, 2005), pp. 30-33, and for a detailed account of a Midlands provincial investigation carried out by Bow Street detectives see Cox, David J., *The Dunsley Murder of 1812: a study in early nineteenth-century crime detection, justice and punishment* (Kingswinford: Dulston Press, 2003).

26. *Annual Register* vol. 9 (1766) p. 138.

27. Anon., *The Merry Thought, or, the Glass-Window and Bog-House Miscellany* (London, *c.*1731), published on the Internet at www.immortalia.com.html. Human and animal waste had been a useful commodity for centuries in the curing and tanning of leather; such public toilets were therefore probably an economic venture as much as a philanthropic gesture.

28. Shropshire Archives P54/L/12/8 Notice to the Overseers of the Poor at Cardington, 1741.

29. Shropshire Archives P60/L/1/1 Appointment of Overseers of the Poor, 1791.

30. Shropshire Archives P28/L/3/1 Article of Agreement to provide Workhouse, 1750.

31. Shropshire Archives BB F/5/5/4 Case for the opinion of Thomas Pemberton, 1794.

32. Shropshire Archives BB F/3/2/55/48 f2 Letter from Thomas Dukes, Vicar of Halesowen, 29 October 1709.

33. 'Some Leaves from the records of the Court of Quarter Sessions for the County of Salop', *Transactions of Shropshire Archaeological Society 2nd series vol iii*, pp. 209-236, p. 215.

34. Quoted in G.C. Baugh, 'County Government 1714-1834', *VCH: Shropshire*, 1979, III, pp. 115-34, p. 130.

35. Page, Lee, *Justice of the Peace* (London: Faber & Faber, 1967), p. 21.

Chapter 4 Policing, Punishment and Social Institutions in the 19th century: the role of the Shropshire Magistracy

1. G.C. Baugh (ed.) *Victoria County Histories – A History of Shropshire*, Volume III (Oxford: Oxford University Press (for Institute of Historical Research, 1979), from now referred to as *VCH: Shropshire*, 1979, III, p. 136.
2. *Ibid.*
3. *Ibid.*, p. 136-7.
4. Kelly's *Directory of Shropshire*, 1863, pp. 643-644; Kelly's *Directory of Shropshire*, 1870, pp. 6-7.
5. *VCH: Shropshire*, 1979, III, p137. By 1885 there were 207 acting magistrates in the county, *ibid.*, p. 136.
6. *Ibid.*, p. 139.
7. The Hon. Richard Noel-Hill (4th Lord Berwick 1842), Henry Burton, H. C. Cotton, J.O. Hopkins, Daniel Nihill (*VCH: Shropshire*, 1979, III, p. 138).
8. *VCH: Shropshire*, 1979, III, p. 138.
9. *Ibid.*, p. 138.
10. Shropshire Quarter Sessions Orders, Vol. IV, 1840-1889, R. Ll. Kenyon, undated, piii; *VCH: Shropshire,* 1979, III, p. 139.
11. *VCH: Shropshire,* 1979, III, p. 139.
12. Diary 2 July 1855, quoted in Walsh, V.J. 'The Diary of a Country Gentleman: Sir Baldwin Leighton Bt., *Transactions of the Shropshire Archaeological Society*, Vol. LIX, p. 159.
13. *VCH: Shropshire,* 1979, III, p. 140.
14. *Ibid.* pp. 140-141. Hill and Leighton were both Conservatives.
15. *Ibid.* pp. 141.
16. Chairman of Finance Committee, 1856-1860.
17. Chairman of the Police Committee, 1864-1866.
18. Chairman of Visiting Justices of Asylum, 1855-1877.
19. Chairman of the Police Committee, 1858-1861, also Chairman of Judges' House Committee 1855-1859.
20. *VCH: Shropshire,* 1979, III, p. 142.
21. *Ibid.* pp. 142-143.
22. Philips, 'Black Country', p. 166.
23. R.E. Swift, 'The English Urban Magistracy and the Administration of Justice during the Early Nineteenth Century: Wolverhampton 1815-1860', *Midland History*, Vol. 17, 1992, p. 90.
24. D. Foster, 'Class and County Government in Early Nineteenth Century Lancashire, *Northern History*, Vol. 9, 1974, p. 60.
25. Swift, 'English Urban', p. 90.
26. *VCH: Shropshire, 1979, III*, p. 141.
27. *Ibid.*, p. 141.
28. V.J. Walsh, 'Old and New Poor Laws in Shropshire, 1820-1870', *Midland History*, Vol. 2, No. 4, Autumn 1974, p. 232.
29. *Ibid.* p. 238.
30. *Ibid.*; MH 32/15, 23 April 1838 quoted in ibid. p. 238.
31. Walsh, 'Old and New', pp. 238-239.
32. *Ibid.* p. 239.
33. *Ibid.* p. 239.
34. *Ibid.* p. 239. Walsh uses three indices to measure quality of life: the repairs and construction of the physical premises, the educational care afforded the children and the dietaries fed to all inmates, see Walsh, 'Poor Law', pp. 204-279.

35. Walsh, 'Old and New', p. 241.
36. *Ibid.* p. 241.
37. *VCH: Shropshire,* 1979, III, p. 160.
38. Walsh, 'Diary', pp. 152-153.
39. *VCH: Shropshire,* 1979, III, p. 160.
40. Walsh, 'Diary', p. 153.
41. *Ibid.* pp. 153-154.
42. *Ibid.* p. 154.
43. *Ibid.* p. 154.
44. *VCH: Shropshire,* 1979, III, p. 160.
45. *Ibid.* p. 161.
46. John Bather (1819-1886), of Dayhouse, Meole Brace, Lord of the Manor and Patron of Meole Brace, MA and Fellow of St. John's College, Cambridge, Burke's *Landed Gentry*, Vol. 1, 1898, p. 84.
47. Moses George Benson (1797-1871) of Lutwyche Hall, JP and Deputy Lieutenant for Shropshire and Worcestershire, Burke's *Landed Gentry*, Vol. 1, 1898, pp. 97-98.
48. *VCH: Shropshire,* 1979, III, p. 161.
49. C. Emsley, *Crime and Society in England, 1750-1900* (Essex: Longman, 1996), p. 216.
50. C. Emsley, *The English Police: A Political and Social History* (Essex : Longman, 1991), pp. 42-43.
51. D. Philips & R. Storch, *Policing Provincial England, 1829-1856 The Politics of Reform* (London: Leicester University Press, 1999), p. 33.
52. *Ibid.* p. 37.
53. HO 73/2/1 B. Leighton to E. Chadwick, 27th February 1839 quoted in *ibid.* p. 49. Philips & Storch, *Policing*, p. 111; Rawlings, P., *Policing: A Short History*, (Cullompton: Willan, 2002), p. 132.
54. Philips & Storch, *Policing*, p. 106.
55. *Ibid.* p. 106.
56. *Ibid.* p. 107.
57. *Shropshire Chronicle* and *Shrewsbury Chronicle*, 4 January 1839 quoted in *ibid.* p. 107.
58. D.J. Elliot, *Policing Shropshire 1836-1967* (Studley, Warwickshire: Brewin Books, 1984), p. 14.
59. Philips & Storch, *Policing*, p. 108.
60. Quoted *ibid.* p. 108.
61. QSF/27/24 quoted *ibid.* pp. 108-109.
62. *Ibid.* p. 108.
63. *Ibid.* p136.
64. *Ibid.* p. 136.
65. *Ibid.* p. 161.
66. *VCH: Shropshire,* 1979, III, p. 142.
67. These were the Chairman and the Deputy Chairman of the Quarter Sessions and the chairman of the three other main committees, Finance, Visitors of the Asylum, Visiting Justices of the Prison, *ibid.*, p. 144.
68. *Ibid.*
69. D.J. Elliot, *Policing Shropshire 1836-1967* (Studley, Warwickshire: Brewin Books, 1984), p. 67.
70. J. Howard, *The State of the Prisons in England and Wales* (Warrington: Warrington Press, 1784), pp. 353-355.
71. *Ibid.* p. 355.
72. *Ibid.* p. 356.

73. *VCH: Shropshire*, 1979, III, p. 125.

74. J.L. Hobbs, *Shrewsbury Street Names* (John Thornhill: Shrewsbury, 1982), p. 63.

75. *VCH: Shropshire*, 1979, III, p. 126.

76. Shropshire Archives QA 2/1/1, Visiting Justices Reports (VJR), p. 128, p. 131.

77. Some commentators were particularly concerned about the damaging effects that the separate system could have on the minds of prisoners, see H. Johnston, '"Buried Alive": Representations of the separate system in Victorian England' in P. Mason (ed.) *Captured by the Media: Prison discourse in media culture*, (Willan, forthcoming).

78. Shropshire Archives QA 2/1/2, VJR, p. 110.

79. *Ibid.*

80. Shropshire Archives QA 2/1/4, VJR, p. 154.

81. S. McConville, 'The Victorian Prison: England, 1865-1965' in N. Morris and D.J. Rothman (eds.) *The Oxford History of the Prison – The Practice of Punishment in Western Society* (Oxford: Oxford University Press, 1998), pp. 131-132.

82. These are the magistrates who were appointed at least ten times as visiting justices to the prison in the documents available (sixty-eight lists of justices appointed between Oct. 1845 and Dec. 1877). The records are complete between the years 1859 and 1877.

83. S. & B. Webb, *English Local Government – The Parish and the County*, Volume One (London: Frank Cass & Co., 1963), pp. 286-7.

84. For example, Revd. Henry Burton and Revd. Edward Warter were also visitors at Shelton Lunatic Asylum.

85. For more discussion see H. Johnston, 'The Shropshire Magistracy', forthcoming; H. Johnston, 'Transformations of Imprisonment in a local context: A case study of Shrewsbury in the nineteenth century, Unpublished Ph.D. thesis, Keele University, 2004.

86. P. King & J. Noel 'The Origins of '"The Problem of Juvenile Delinquency": the growth of juvenile prosecutions in London in the late 18th and early 19th centuries,' *Criminal Justice History : An International Annual*, 14, 1994, pp. 17.

87. *Ibid.*

88. *Ibid.* p18. When and why this transition took place is of much debate, see King & Noel 'Origins'; M. May, 'Innocence and Experience: The Evolution of the Concept of Juvenile Delinquency in the Mid-Nineteenth Century', *Victorian Studies*, 17, 1, 1973, pp. 7-29; S. Magarey, 'The Invention of Juvenile Delinquency in Early Nineteenth Century London', *Labour History*, 34, 1978, pp. 11-25; H. Shore, *Artful Dodgers: Youth and Crime in Early 19th-Century London* (Woodbridge: Boydell Press, 2002).

89. May 'Innocence and Experience', p. 11.

90. Shropshire Archives QA 2/1/3, VJR, p37.

91. S. McConville, *A History of Prison Administration, 1750-1877,* Volume One (London : Routledge Kegan Paul, 1981), p. 333.

92. Brougham Committee quoted in McConville, *Prison Administration*, p. 334.

93. The Philanthropic Society Farm School was established in Redhill, Surrey in 1848 and became a model for many of the reformatory schools established in England and Wales in the 1850s and 1860s (Magarey 'Invention', p. 1).

94. Shropshire Archives QA 2/1/3, VJR, pp. 109-110.

95. *Ibid.* p. 111.

96. The 1835 Select Committee on Gaols had recommended the establishment of a juvenile prison. Parkhurst prison for boys opened in 1838. The overwhelming majority of the boys were to be transported but an assessment of the prisoner's performance decided whether he was to be transported as a free emigrant, or under a conditional pardon, or having been deemed incorrigible, to be kept in confinement on arrival. Parkhurst was intended to serve two purposes: to add the deterrent element that transportation was said to lack and to provide

occupational training that would enable fit young convicts, with little or no criminal record, to make a better life for themselves in the colonies (McConville, *Prison Administration*, pp. 204-5). For the Act establishing Parkhurst prison for young offenders see 1 & 2 Vict. c82.

97. Shropshire Archives QA 2/1/3, VJR, pp. 111.
98. *Ibid.* p. 112.
99. *Ibid.* p. 165. Those appointed to the Committee were Sir Baldwin Leighton Bart., W. W. Whitmore Esq., G. Pritchard Esq., T. W. Wylde Browne Esq., Reverend H. Burton and Reverend D. Nihill.
100. *Ibid.* pp. 171-75.
101. *Ibid.* p. 176, p. 177.
102. This was upon a motion of Mr. Wylde Browne, seconded by Wolvyche Whitmore.
103. Shropshire Archives QA 2/1/3, VJR, p. 178.
104. *Ibid.* The petition was signed by Baldwin Leighton V. C, W. W. Whitmore, J. Wylde Browne, G. Pritchard, R. George Jebb, Robert Burton, W. Butler Lloyd, Daniel Nihill, Henry Burton, Henry Justice, George J. Hill, M. G. Benson, H. Homfray and Wm. Haycocks.
105. Shropshire Archives QA 2/1/3, VJR, p. 184.
106. Sir Baldwin Leighton, T. Wylde Browne and William Wolvyche Whitmore were the Committee.
107. Shropshire Archives QA 2/1/3, VJR, p. 189.
108. *Ibid.* p. 204.
109. Shropshire Archives QA 2/1/4, VJR, p. 8.
110. *Ibid.* p. 27.
111. 10 & 11 Vict. c82. This Act changed the way juveniles were tried for simple larceny, all juveniles under the age of 14 were to be tried summarily in a petty sessions court and not on indictment. The Juveniles Offenders Act 1850 extended the age limit to 16. For more discussion of these Acts see D. Taylor, *Crime, Policing and Punishment in England, 1750-1914* (London: Macmillan, 1998).
112. Series 1 indicates a three year moving average.
113. McConville, *Prison Administration*, p. 338.
114. *Ibid.* p. 339.

Chapter 5 The 20th century and beyond: the future of the Bench

1. 'Introduction' to *Notes for New Magistrates of England and Wales* (London: The Magistrates Association, 1961).
2. The Magistrates in the Community Project is supported by the Magistrates' Association and was formally launched in 1995 to increase public awareness of the role of the lay magistracy in the criminal and civil justice systems. Panels of magistrates visit schools, colleges and community groups to give presentations on how the magistracy functions.
3. We would wish to thank Catherine Trimby, Chairman of Shrewsbury Court; Anne Gee, Magistrates Court Committee member and past Chairman of Ludlow Court; Tom Acton, retired Chairman of Ludlow Court; Aubrey de Vere Beauclerk, retired Chairman of Oswestry Court; and Frank Leath OBE, retired Chairman of Shrewsbury Court. The quotations used in this chapter are not attributable to any particular magistrate.
4. Clare Graham has written a comprehensive gazetteer of court houses, arranged by county, with an explanation of how court architecture reflected changing attitudes towards crime and punishment, see C. Graham, *Ordering Law. The architecture and social history of the English law court to 1914* (Aldershot: Ashgate, 2003).
5. Briggs, Harrison, McInnes and Vincent, *Crime and Punishment in England* (London: UCL Press, 1996), p. 207.

6. Muncie, J. and Wilson, D. (eds.), *Student Handbook of criminal justice and Criminology* (London: Cavendish, 2004).

7. See Sir T. Skyrme, *History of the Justices of the Peace* (Chichester: Barry Rose, 1994); P. Seago, C. Walker and D. Wall, *The Role and Appointment of Stipendiary Magistrates* (Leeds: Centre of Criminal Justice Studies, 1995); P. Seago, C. Walker and D. Wall, 'The development of the professional magistracy in England and Wales, *Criminal Law Review*, 2000, 631-651.

8. R. Morgan and N. Russell, *The Judiciary in the Magistrates Courts [Home Office Occasional Paper no. 66]* (London: Home Office, 2000).

9. 'Narey' courts are named after a Home Office official, Martin Narey, who in 1997 produced the *Narey Review of Delay in the Criminal Justice System.*

10. B. Godfrey, Leverhulme Trust Project, 'Sentencing Theory and its use in the Law Courts' (July 2001).

11. Letter to Justices from G.C. Godber, Clerk of the Peace, Shrewsbury, 15th October, 1965

12. *'Introduction' to Notes for New Magistrates of England and Wales* (London: The Magistrates Association, 1961), p. 7.

13. A. De Fonblanque, *How We Are Governed. The Crown, the Senate, and the Bench*, 12th edition, 1871.

14. See, amongst others, P. Carlen and A. Worrall, *Women, Crime and Justice* (Milton Keynes: Open University Press, 1987); P. Carlen, *Women, Crime and Poverty* (Milton Keynes: Open University Press, 1988); P. Darbyshire, 'For the New Lord Chancellor – some causes for concern about magistrates', *Criminal Law Review*, 1997; J. Dignam and A. Wynne, '"A microcosm of the local community?": reflections on the composition of the magistracy in a petty sessional division in the North Midlands', *British Journal of Criminology*, Vol. 3, no. 2, 1997.

15. Paper by the Clerk of the Committee, MCC papers, December 1953.

16. There is now a preference to explore the possibility of the multiple use of courthouses i.e. Probation and County Court using Oswestry's building, the County Court using Ludlow's building, and various options being considered for Shrewsbury.

17. Lord Merthyr, quoted in Skyrme p.30. Skyrme notes that his Lordship later became a stout defender of the lay principle when he was chairman of the Magistrates Association.

18. Royal Commission on Justices of the Peace 1946-48 (Cmd.7463), Minutes of Evidence, October 30th, 1946, q.223.

19. Right Honourable Lord Justice Auld, 'A Review of the Criminal Courts of England and Wales', September 2001, available online at www.criminal-courts-review.org.uk/

20. R. Morgan, 'Trust me, I'm a magistrate: The role of lay persons in judicial decision-making in England and Wales', Australia and New Zealand Criminology Conference, Melbourne, February 2001.

21. R. Morgan and N. Russell, *The Judiciary in the Magistrates Courts* (London: Home Office, 2000).

22. Right Honourable Lord Justice Auld, 'A Review of the Criminal Courts of England and Wales', September 2001; John Halliday, 'The Halliday Review (Making Punishments Work: Review of the Sentencing Framework for England and Wales), October 2001.

Index

Also from Logaston Press

Churches of Shropshire & their Treasures

by John Leonard

This book explores 320 parish churches of Shropshire, half of them medieval. Early chapters guide the reader through changing architectural styles, from Anglo-Saxon origins to the 21st century. Then the author looks more closely at the treasures of the churches, including towers and spires, porches, roofs, sculpture, fonts, memorials and monuments, stained glass, rood-screens, pulpits, pews and chancel furnishings.

The county is then divided into geographical areas, with descriptions of all the individual churches in each area. The author indicates those churches which he considers to be the most rewarding to visit, including a significant number of Victorian churches which are often undervalued.

John Leonard is a retired consultant physician who lives in Hopesay, Shropshire. He has written books on the parish churches of Cheshire, Derbyshire, Herefordshire, Staffordshire and London.

Paperback, 332 pages with over 530 photographs

ISBN 1 904396 19 4   £12.95

Also from Logaston Press

Vernacular Buildings of Shropshire

by Madge Moran

Over a period spanning thirty years, Madge Moran has visited, decyphered and recorded many of Shropshire's vernacular buildings that owe their origins to the period commencing *c.*1200. This book brings together that work, with the exception of the area around Whitchurch which has been covered in the earlier publication *Vernacular Buildings of Whitchurch and Area and their occupants.*

Initial chapters track the changes from buildings designed with defence in mind to first-floor halls of both stone and timber-framing and thence to ground-floor halls. Cruck buildings are given their own chapter, as are box-framed and jettied houses. Roof construction, with its various forms across Shropshire, is also accorded its own section. The changes from the fully developed three-part plan medieval house with its clearly defined solar and service ends or wings, screens passage and open hall to what may be called the 'early modern' house, fully floored, with a central entrance and displaying symmetry to a greater or lesser degree, are covered in a chapter on the Transitional House. Other chapters cover wallpaintings and dendrochronology—the latter an important aspect of Madge Moran's work and which provides much of the dating information in this book.

With a concentration of buildings in Ludlow, Shrewsbury and Much Wenlock that have both survived and provided an opportunity for inspection, these towns are given a series of their own chapters which develop themes specific to each town. The wealth of information relating to other properties spread across Shropshire is recorded in a gazetteer which is organised on a parish basis.

This book provides a series of very readable chapters that tell the story of Shropshire's vernacular buildings, as well as providing an invaluable reference work.

Paperback, 600 pages with over 1,500 drawings and photographs
ISBN: 1 873827 93 8   £25

Also from Logaston Press

English Architecture to 1900: The Shropshire Experience

by Eric Mercer

Eric Mercer's book, originally commissioned by Victoria County History, is a comprehensive guide to Shropshire's architecture, covering church and secular buildings from Anglo-Saxon times to 1900. The range includes Anglican, Catholic and Non-Conformist churches, manor houses and country mansions, the houses of the gentry and yeomanry, town houses, semis and working-class terraces as well as public and communal buildings like railway stations, banks, factories and shops.

Throughout, the intention is to relate regional developments in architecture to a national pattern, to show whether and where Shropshire architecture was in advance of or behind national trends and what distinctive local themes and styles developed. Eric Mercer traces patrons and owners to show how the sources of their wealth, their social aspirations and their political ambitions were the main determinants of the forms of their houses and the nature of their decoration. Ecclesiastical architecture and the styles of public and communal buildings are likewise explained in terms of their social functions and political objectives.

This book has been eagerly awaited. Eric Mercer's encyclopaedic knowledge and unique styles of analysis are used to encapsulate his ideas, not only about Shropshire's architecture, but about making the study of architecture a vital ingredient in an understanding of the broad historical context. In relating the Shropshire experience to national development, he produces a book which not only chronicles the progress of English architecture, but the march of English history, each serving to illuminate and enrich an understanding of the other.

Eric Mercer was a leading authority on English buildings and a pioneer of the study of the history of vernacular architecture.

Paperback, 400 pages with over 300 photographs, drawings and plans
ISBN: 1 904396 08 9   £20

Also from Logaston Press

The Folklore of Shropshire

by Roy Palmer

Shropshire's folklore is presented in a series of themed chapters that encompass landscape, buildings, beliefs, work, seasons, people, music and drama. In the eleven chapters the county's rich store of folklore unfolds in a way that allows you to dip into what most intrigues, or to read from start to finish. Here are stories of mark stones, stone circles, giants, tunnels, dragons, rivers, meres, pools, hills, church sites changed by the devil, vengeful spirits, bull and bear baiting, cockfighting, fairs, herbal remedies and those which involve peculiar activities, minstrels, histriones, waits, charmers and 'cunning folk', ghosts, witches, bountiful cows, of characters such as the early saints, Caratacus, Edric the Wild, Humphrey Kynaston, Jack Mytton and even recent folklore surrounding Hilda Murrell, of tales of the Civil War and of Hopton Quarter, of celebrations and customs surrounding times such as Easter, Christmas, All Souls' Eve, Ascension Day and Palm Sunday along with the likes of 'burning the mawkin', 'tin panning' and wife selling, of rhymes that link villages, ballads that tell of events in the county's past, of folk plays and mummers—to mention just some of what is included.

Roy Palmer is nationally known for his researches into folklore and with Logaston Press has recently published *The Folklore of Radnorshire*, *The Folklore of (old) Monmouthshire* (reflecting the original size of the county) and *Herefordshire Folklore*. In addition he has written on the folklore of Gloucestershire and also of his native Leicestershire. The anthologies he has edited include *A Taste of Ale* and *Boxing the Compass*. In 2004 he was awarded the English Folk Dance and Song Society's highest honour, its gold badge.

Paperback, 320 pages with over 250 photographs,
drawings and samples of music

ISBN 1 904396 16 X   £12.95